THE New Public Service

CENTER FOR PUBLIC SERVICE

Brookings Institution established the Center for Public Service in 1999 to answer three simple questions: what is the state of the public service today, how can the public sector issue a more compelling invitation to serve, and how can the public sector be a wise steward of the talent it recruits? The Center for Public Service espouses the simple belief that effective governance is impossible if public agencies, be they government or nonprofit, cannot compete for their fair share of talent in an increasingly tight labor market. Interested in more than basic research, the center aims to develop and disseminate pragmatic ideas that, if put to the test, will improve the odds that more talented Americans will enter the public service.

As part of this effort, the Center for Public Service has set forth an aggressive agenda to include a series of publications and reports, conferences, and other public events in order to encourage young Americans to enter the public service and to instill in all Americans a greater sense of confidence and integrity in that service. As with all Brookings publications, the judgments, conclusions, and recommendations presented in the studies are solely those of the authors and should not be attributed to the trustees, officers, or other staff members of the institution.

THE New Public Service

PAUL C. LIGHT

BROOKINGS INSTITUTION PRESS
Washington, D.C.

BODO0609-9/2

Copyright © 1999
THE BROOKINGS INSTITUTION
1775 Massachusetts Avenue, N.W.,
Washington, D.C. 20036
www.brookings.edu

Library of Congress Cataloging-in-Publication data
Light, Paul Charles.
  The new public service / Paul C. Light.
    p.   cm.
  Includes bibliographical references and index.
  ISBN 0-8157-5243-1 (pbk. : alk. paper)
  1. Civil service—United States. 2. United States—Officials and
employees—Interviews. 3. Public administration—United States.
I. Title.
  JK692 .L537 1999   99-006972
  352.6'3'0973—dc21   CIP

          9 8 7 6 5 4 3 2 1

The paper used in this publication meets minimum requirements of the American
National Standard for Information Sciences—Permanence of Paper for Printed
Library Materials: ANSI Z39.48-1984.

Typeset in Sabon

Composition by R. Lynn Rivenbark
Macon, Georgia

Printed by Automated Graphic Systems
White Plains, Maryland

To James E. Jernberg,
the finest educator of public servants I have known

FOREWORD

This report provides a first glimpse of what Paul C. Light defines as the new public service. It is a public service committed to making a difference wherever that difference can be made, be it in government, nonprofit agencies, or private firms. And it is a public service that is ready to switch sectors to find the impact it desires. At least for graduates of this nation's most prestigious public policy and administration schools, Light argues that the thirty-year government career is mostly a thing of the past, replaced by careers with far greater mobility and challenge than ever before.

Light is not interested in calling for a return to the good old days. Rather, he is primarily concerned with cataloging the changes, giving the graduates he interviewed a chance to talk about why they have taken their different paths, and providing advice to the graduate schools, their students, and their students' future employers on how to embrace what has become a multisectored, fast-changing public service. He believes that the new public service is here to stay, forged in part by the political pressures to reduce government employment, as well as the very real advantages of using nonprofit and private agencies to provide services once delivered by government employees.

At the same time, Light also believes that government must become much more competitive if it is to maintain its core capacity in what has become a public-service labor shortage. It must not only do a better job of inviting talented Americans to service, but also must make that service much more attractive. The search for pragmatic reforms in how government recruits and deploys its human capital is the central focus of the new Center for Public Service. It also reflects a longstanding Brookings commitment to making government work.

The research that undergirds this report could not have been collected without the participation of the thirteen graduate programs that provided the alumni lists from which the sample of 1,000 graduates was drawn, as well as the graduates who agreed to be interviewed for the project, including some who may have taken Light's courses during his tenure as a professor at the University of Minnesota's Humphrey Institute of Public Affairs. Nor could the research have been conducted without the creative energies and survey expertise of Princeton Survey Research Associates and its principal investigator, Mary McIntosh, and her talented staff. Light is also grateful for the special insights of his own research team at Brookings, particularly his research assistants Kristen Lippert-Martin and Philippe Rosse, and for vigilant questioning by Carole Plowfield. He thanks as well the efforts of the Brookings Institution Press, including Carlotta Ribar, who edited the manuscript, Mary Mortensen, who provided the index, and Eloise C. Stinger, who proofread the pages.

The final report clearly benefited from input by Light's colleagues at several of the leading schools, including Harvard University's John F. Kennedy School of Government and Syracuse University's Maxwell School. In particular, Light thanks Deans Joseph S. Nye and Herman "Dutch" Leonard at the Kennedy School, and Deans John Palmer and Astrid Merget at Maxwell. He also extends his appreciation to the faculty of the University of Delaware School of Public Administration for providing early feedback on the findings, and the many colleagues who acted as a sounding board on the project. He especially thanks Dean Walter Broadnax of American University, Barbara Nelson of the University of California, Los Angeles, Judith Feder of Georgetown University, and Rosslyn Kleeman of George Washington University.

This report could not have been written without the support of the Dillon Fund, which endowed Light's chair in honor of Douglas Dillon and also provided the funding to underwrite Light's research activities. The Center for Public Service also received support for portions of this work from the Ford Foundation. Finally, Light thanks Rebecca

W. Rimel and his former staff at the Pew Charitable Trusts for enduring his early explorations of this topic and for supporting much of the research on which this report is based, including its continued support for the Pew Research Center for the People and the Press. Pew has been a leader in both asking the hard questions about the current state of American democracy and supporting the rigorous research needed to provide the answers.

The views expressed here are those of the author and should not be ascribed to persons or organizations acknowledged above, or to the trustees, officers, and other staff members of the Brookings Institution.

MICHAEL H. ARMACOST
President

November 1999

CONTENTS

1 The Changing Shape of Government   1

2 Paths into Service   19

3 A Profile of the Profession   42

4 Educating the New Public Service   103

5 Embracing the New Public Service   125

Appendixes

A Survey Methodology   143

B Survey Questionnaire   148

Notes   167

Index   181

THE New
Public Service

1

THE CHANGING SHAPE
OF GOVERNMENT

This report is about the end of the government-centered public service and the rise of a multisectored service to replace it. Designed to sustain thirty-year careers with one way in at the entry level and one way out at retirement, the government-centered public service is increasingly unattractive to a work force that will change jobs and sectors frequently, and to workers who are much more focused on challenging work than security. Gone are the days when talented employees would endure hiring delays and a mind-numbing application process to get an entry-level government job. Gone, too, are the days when talented employees would accept slow but steady advancement through towering government bureaucracies in exchange for a thirty-year commitment. In the midst of a growing labor shortage, government is becoming an employer of last resort, one that caters more to the security-craver than the risk-taker.

Simply stated, young Americans are no longer willing to wait patiently for the chance to accomplish something worthwhile. Having set annual volunteering records in college, they want tangible impacts on the job.[1] If that means a job with a private firm or nonprofit agency, so be it. The government-centered public service has been replaced by a new public service in which government must compete for talent. Unfortunately, as this report will argue, government in general, and the federal government in specific, simply is not configured to offer the work that young Americans want. Battered by downsizing, political scandal, and a never-ending war on waste, the federal government has yet to articulate a clear vision of how to compete against the private sector for talent. Agencies are struggling just to hold the talent they already have, let alone imagine a new public service in which expertise moves more freely across the sectors.

The fact that the erosion of talent is imperceptible does not make it less threatening to democratic life. Ultimately, effective governance is impossible if government cannot attract talented citizens to serve at all levels of the hierarchy. As Alexander Hamilton warned two hundred years ago in *The Federalist Papers,* "a government ill executed, whatever it may be in theory, must be in practice a bad government." Citizens cannot have confidence in the integrity of the democratic process if their leaders cannot honor the promises they make, but those leaders cannot honor the promises they make if government cannot attract the talent necessary to both draft and execute the laws. Much as Americans complain about the size of government, and much as they believe that the federal government creates more problems than it solves, they also expect it to deliver high performance in their favorite programs, whatever their favorites might be.[2]

The federal government's problem in competing for talent is twofold. First, its current hiring system for recruiting talent, top to bottom, underwhelms at almost every task it undertakes. It is slow in the hiring, almost useless in the firing, overly permissive in the promoting, out of touch with actual performance in the rewarding, penurious in the training, and utterly absent in the managing of a vast and hidden work force of contractors and consultants who work side by side, desk by desk with the civil service. Sad to say, when young Americans are asked to picture themselves in public service careers, particularly at the federal level, they picture themselves in deadend jobs where seniority, not performance, rules. And when more seasoned Americans are asked to picture themselves in appointive office, they picture themselves in a nomination and confirmation process characterized by endless inspection, over-disclosure, and delays at both ends of Pennsylvania Avenue.

Second, government appears to be less and less able to provide the kind of work that today's labor market expects. There is no question, for example, that young Americans are more lightly attached to work than previous generations, nor that the most talented among them can demand more from their employers. The civil service system may have mostly stood still since 1978, but the culture of work has changed dramatically, in no small part due to downsizing and corporate mergers.[3] The best available evidence suggests that government is not even winning the battle among young people who have already made the decision to spend their careers serving the public—those battles are being won by private firms and nonprofit agencies.

Contrary to conventional wisdom, there is little evidence that government can win the recruiting battle with higher pay. Pay is no doubt important as students consider first jobs, but it is far less important than the nature of the job itself. Young Americans are not saying "Show me the money" so much as "Show me the work." And it is on that count that government is losing ground.

The Quiet Crisis Continues

This is hardly the first report to document the decline of the public service. Concerns about the continuing problems in recruiting and retaining government talent eventually led to creation of the National Commission on the Public Service, which was chaired by former Federal Reserve Board chairman Paul Volcker. Convened only a decade after the enactment of the Civil Service Reform Act of 1978, the commission assembled the best available data in describing a "quiet crisis" in the federal service.[4]

The term *quiet crisis* was a nearly perfect description of the slow weakening of the public service in the 1970s and 1980s. By the end of the 1980s, the gap between federal and private pay had widened, attacks on government by the media and political candidates were at an all-time high, the Office of Personnel Management had been weakened by a director who believed that mediocre was good enough for government, and the public had lost confidence in its elected and appointed leaders.[5] At the same time, America's most talented citizens had lost interest in public service of any kind, and morale within the civil service was at a modern low. The only problem with the crisis was that it was profoundly quiet. "This erosion has been gradual,

almost imperceptible, year by year," the Volcker Commission concluded. "But it has occurred nonetheless."[6] Not since the time of
Andrew Jackson's spoils system did civil servants have such good reason to feel beleaguered.

The crisis may have been building for years, but its impact on the
public service was unmistakable. As the commission put it: "too many
of the best of the nation's senior executives are ready to leave government, and not enough of its most talented young people are willing to
join. This erosion in the attractiveness of the public service at all
levels—most specifically in the federal civil service—undermines the
ability of government to respond effectively to the needs and aspira-
tions of the American people, and ultimately damages the democratic
process itself."[7]

In retrospect, the commission's report marks a last-gasp effort to
rescue the old public service in what was already becoming a new
labor market. Unfortunately, the commission did not, could not,
anticipate the dramatic restructuring of government that has occurred
since the end of the cold war, a restructuring that has included a massive downsizing of federal employment and a steady blurring of the
lines among government, private, and nonprofit delivery of services.[8]
The symptoms of crisis may have remained unchanged since Volcker,
but the causes and, therefore, the solutions most certainly have not.

There can be little doubt that the quiet crisis continues. Public trust
in government continues to fall, the senior levels of the hierarchy continues to thicken, and young people continue to express significant
doubts about the value of a public service career. If asked to revisit its
opening assessment of the state of the public service, the commission
would find plenty of evidence of continued erosion despite the modest
gain. The erosion remains gradual, almost imperceptible, but it continues nonetheless. It is most certainly time for a reassessment, both of
the underlying problems and the potential solutions, and a fresh assessment of how the public service might be strengthened. This reassessment must confront the growing evidence that government must do
more than merely become more effective at inviting talented citizens to
serve. It must also make that service much more inviting at all levels.

Nor is there much doubt that talented Americans are turning away
from the government-centered public service. Start at the entry level,
where the federal government has become an increasingly unattractive
employer for the nation's top college graduates. Fewer than one in ten

of the 1998 Phi Beta Kappa graduates surveyed by George Washington University rated the federal government as their first preference for an employer, while nearly six in ten said they would not know how to get a federal job even if they wanted one, and nine in ten said that the process for getting a federal job would be long and burdensome.[9]

Even students who have decided to make public service the focus of their life's work are no longer drawn to government first. Just 53 percent of the 1998 public administration students also surveyed by George Washington University ranked government as their first preference for an employer, with the federal government barely outdrawing state and local government, whereas the rest saw their future outside traditional government posts, with the private sector at 27 percent and nonprofits at 22 percent.[10]

Look next inside government, where there is growing evidence that federal employees are finding their work less rewarding. A 1996 Merit Systems Protection Board random-sample survey of nearly 10,000 federal workers found a mix of satisfaction and frustration. The good news is that four out of five respondents were satisfied with their jobs, three out of five would recommend the federal government as a place to work, and most felt pay was adequate. The bad news is that the vast majority of respondents said that the budget cuts, downsizing, and back-to-back government shutdowns in 1995 had a negative impact on their organizations, and four out of ten said that fears of future reductions in force were having a continued, negative impact on productivity.[11]

This general blend of satisfaction and frustration continues up the hierarchy to the most senior elected and appointed positions. On the one hand, a recent survey of members of Congress, presidential appointees, and career senior executives shows significant job satisfaction; 57 percent of the members of Congress, 64 percent of presidential appointees, and 56 percent of the career members of the Senior Executive Service report that they are very satisfied. Most also say they are more satisfied today than they were when they first started in their jobs.

On the other hand, all three groups of leaders report greater frustration with actually doing their jobs. Political appointees work long hours under great media scrutiny. Although they say they are willing to work as long as it takes, they also report enormous frustration at the amount of time they have to spend in administering antiquated systems and testifying before Congress on what they see as trivial issues. All three groups complain mightily about not having enough time to work on policy—members of Congress are particularly frustrated with campaign fund-raising, while presidential appointees and senior executives appear desperate to be freed from doing routine administrative tasks and responding to congressional requests.[12]

Overall, the evidence suggests that government has lost whatever competitive edge it might have had in the 1970s in recruiting talented Americans to service. On the whole, government jobs are not particularly inviting these days, nor are agencies doing much inviting. It is still mostly up to talented employees to find government, not vice versa. And there is still mostly just one way into a government job right after high school or college, and mostly just one way out twenty to thirty years later at retirement.

What may make the current state of the public service more troubling is the entry of a mostly new competitor for talent: the private contractors that are delivering more and more of the nation's public services.[13] Anecdotal reports from the leading public policy and administration schools suggests a significant increase in recruiting pressure from these firms, which do more than just outbid government on entry-level pay and benefits, even as they offer five-figure signing bonuses. They can also out-recruit government on campus, providing a much more polished image of their organizations than does government. They can also offer the opportunity for rapid advancement in growing federal, state, and local government practices.

The challenge for further analysis is less to define the nature of the problem than to understand its origins and potential solutions. Nor is it just to recycle past ideas for rescuing the thirty-year government career, as so many reformers do in nostalgic calls for renewal. Although there is no doubt that the old public service can be strengthened, the current reform proposals ignore the fundamental changes in the market of potential public servants, a market that has become much more deliberate in the search for meaningful work.

Searching for the New Public Service

Beyond the accounts cited above, there is little systematic evidence on the rise of the new public service. One can only infer its rise through the movement of jobs from government to private firms and nonprofit agencies as Congress and the president have simultaneously downsized the federal work force and devolved responsibilities to states, localities, and nonprofit agencies over the past two decades.

Between 1984 and 1996, for example, the federal government cut roughly 1.6 million full-time-equivalent positions from its combined work force of civil servants, uniformed military personnel, postal workers, contractors, and grantees. Remove the Department of Defense and its massive downsizing from the figures, however, and the true size of the federal work force actually grew from 5.5 million to 6.3 million during the period, including a dramatic increase in the number of positions created under contracts for services. Even at Defense, where the end of the cold war brought an estimated loss of roughly 2.5 million jobs (civilian, military, contractors, and grantees), the service contract work force actually increased by 100,000 jobs, rising from 2.2 million in 1984 to 2.3 million twelve years later. At non-Defense agencies, the increase in service jobs was even more dramatic, rising from 1.3 million to 1.7 million.

Outsourcing fever also hit the state and local levels of government, where private firms are competing for a growing share of public work in managing everything from prisons (Corrections Corporation of America) to welfare (Lockheed Martin). According to William Ryan, "the real news is not the appearance of a few high-profile for-profit players on the field but rather the underlying changes that have made their entry and rapid growth possible. While many nonprofits are still reeling from cutbacks on social spending, for-profits are celebrating the fact that government outsourcing is still growing in so many areas."[14] From San Diego, California, where Lockheed Martin, Maximus, and Catholic Charities deliver welfare-to-work services on the city's behalf, to Dade County, Florida, where Lockheed Martin is the paymaster for roughly thirty nonprofits providing those same services for the county, the private sector is getting ever more deeply involved in doing work once done by government. And just who is doing the work for Lockheed Martin? Former government and nonprofit executives who are moving to the big paychecks, leaving a deforested public sector in their wake.

The Changing Shape of Government

The past fifteen years have witnessed the most dramatic, yet least understood, reshaping of the administrative state in U.S. history. During the Clinton administration alone, the federal government reduced its civil service work force by a sixth (191,000 jobs), eliminated a quarter of its middle-level management positions (35,000 jobs), and sliced its Defense contract work force by nearly a third (1.6 million jobs). At the same time, it increased its non-Defense contract and grant work force by a sixth (600,000 jobs). In 1997, for the first time in civil service history, employees at the middle level of government outnumbered those at the lower levels (638,427 to 594,126).

These changes have clearly altered the traditional government-centered nature of public service. Simply stated, as go the jobs, so goes the public service. Viewed in hierarchical terms, for example, the federal government has become more circular, even elliptical, over time. More and more federal employees are doing the supervising and procuring of work from nonfederal employees, who are doing the delivering and producing. Part of the shift reflects the natural evolution of work. The bottom of government has been slimming for decades as new technologies have rendered frontline jobs obsolete. Under unrelenting political pressure to keep the civil service small, agencies have done what comes naturally: push as much front-line work outward and downward as possible.

As I argue in *The True Size of Government*, most of that slimming was a product of attrition-based downsizing and the lack of clear guidelines for deciding which jobs should stay inside government and which should go.[15] It stretches credulity, for example, to argue that nearly 191,000 lower-level jobs suddenly became obsolete in 1993. The federal government eliminated primarily the jobs that were the easiest to cut, meaning the ones with the highest attrition and the lowest political profile.

The rest of the federal pyramid, and much of the new public service, will still exist in this elliptical future. It will just reside outside of the federal headcount in the millions of people who will work for contractors, grantees, and state and local governments delivering services on the federal government's behalf. As long as the federal mission continues to grow, and there are few hints that it will do otherwise, the faithful execution of the laws will rely more on writing careful contracts, grants, and mandates than on the traditional chain of command between elected representatives and the career work force below. And, in turn, the execution of those contracts, grants, and mandates will fall less to federal employees and much more to a new public service increasingly composed of employees who divide their loyalties and careers between the sectors as they look for work that matters.

The changing shape of the federal government can be seen in its girth, height, and mix of jobs. Its girth has been tightening, thereby reducing opportunities for hiring at all levels; its height has been growing, thereby burnishing its unenviable reputation as an over-layered, frustrating place to work; and its bottom has been disappearing as frontline jobs have been contracted out to the private and nonprofit sectors.

GIRTH. The tightening girth of government can be seen throughout the hierarchy, starting with the very top of government, where presidential appointees and senior career executives work. According to the Winter 1998 edition of the *Federal Yellow Book*, 2,462 federal executives carried some variation of the five top titles in a federal government department: secretary, deputy secretary, under secretary, assistant secretary, and administrator. That number includes everything from chiefs of staffs to associate under secretaries, assistant inspectors general to principal deputy administrators. That figure had increased more than fivefold from 1960 to 1993.

To its credit, the Clinton administration held the total number of executives in check. Those 2,462 officials represent an addition of just fifty-four since January 20, 1993, including seventy-eight jobs in the newly independent Social Security Administration. Subtract those positions from the count, and the executive corps actually lost weight. In contrast, the Reagan administration added 173 posts to the top of government, while the Bush administration added over 600.[16]

Also to its credit, the Clinton administration reduced the number of middle managers. The federal government employed 126,000 middle managers in 1997, down from 161,000 in 1992, 150,000 in 1989, but roughly equal to the number of middle managers in 1983. The government employed eight rank-and-file workers for every supervisor in 1993; by 1997 the ratio was eleven to one. Moreover, all but two departments lost mid-level supervisors. Only Justice (up roughly 2,000 supervisors) and State (up 18) increased the number of mid-level managers, while Interior and Treasury each lost roughly a sixth; Agriculture, Commerce, Labor, and Transportation almost a fifth; Education and the General Services Administration more than a third; the Environmental Protection Agency and Housing and Urban Development almost two-fifths; Energy and the National Aeronautics and Space Administration more than half; and the Office of Personnel Management more than two-thirds.[17]

The cuts in middle management were part of a governmentwide reduction in total employment that began in 1989 when Congress ordered the closing of the first of what would become 243 obsolete military bases, accelerated in 1993 when Clinton ordered a 100,000 cut in total federal employment, and culminated with a total cut of 272,900 under the Workforce Restructuring Act of 1994. Although the number of political appointees and senior executives remained constant and management accounted for just 10 percent of the downsizing, the Clinton administration was able to reverse a two-decade rise in the numbers of both senior- and middle-level managers.

HEIGHT. Although the number of senior executives and middle managers remained steady during the 1990s, the number of layers they occupy did not. At the middle levels, for example, many agencies reduced the number of managers by merely assigning different titles. According to the General Accounting Office, 41 percent of the downsizing of supervisors at the NASA Marshall Space Flight Center in Huntsville, Alabama, involved such reclassification, as did 40 percent of the cuts at the Bureau of Land Management and 35 percent at the Federal Aviation Administration. The Social Security Administration cut nearly 2,800 middle-level supervisory titles from 1993 to 1998 but created 1,900 new nonsupervisory titles, including 500 team leaders and 1,350 management support specialists.

The continued layering of government is most apparent at the top. There, the Clinton administration clearly failed to stem the generation of new titles. Indeed, it witnessed the most significant addition of layers in modern executive history. From 1993 to 1998, the fourteen departments of government created sixteen new senior-level titles, including a stunning number of new *alter ego* deputy posts, including deputy to the deputy secretary, principal assistant deputy under secretary, associate principal deputy assistant secretary, chief of staff to the under secretary, assistant chief of staff to the administrator, and chief of staff to the assistant administrator. Government's top tier may not have grown wider, but it most certainly grew taller.

The Clinton layering would have been even greater had three titles not disappeared along the way: principal associate deputy under secretary (which had existed in the Department of Energy), associate deputy under secretary (which had existed in six departments and appears to have moved up into the deputy secretary position), and associate assistant administrator (twelve of which had existed in the Department of Commerce). In total, the Clinton administration created nineteen new titles and removed three, yielding a net increase of sixteen, allowing the creation of as many new titles during its first six years as the past seven administrations created over the preceding thirty-three years.

Not all of the new layers will hold, however. Only five of the new titles exist in more than one department to date; most of the new titles are held by only one person in one department. But if the past is prologue, many of the titles will spread to other departments, largely through a process that sociologists label as isomorphism and that Senator Daniel Patrick Moynihan calls the "iron law of emulation." Except for the secretary title, which has existed since the first Congress created the first department, each title in the phone book originated in only one department.

Whatever the underlying incentive for title copying, the layering increases the distance that ideas must travel up to reach the secretary, and guidance must travel down to the frontlines of government. More hands must touch the paper, more signatures grace the page, and more eyes read the memos. It is impossible for the top to know what the bottom is doing when the bottom remains thirty, forty, or more layers below; it is impossible for the bottom to hear the top when messages go through dozens of interpretations on their journey down. Like the childhood game of "telephone," in which messages become hopelessly distorted as they are relayed from child to child, the layers merely add to the potential confusion and loss of accountability between the top and the bottom.

JOB MIX. Presidential appointees and senior managers were not alone in surviving the downsizing mostly untouched. The middle levels of government also remained intact. Although the number of middle-level managers fell by a quarter, the number of middle level nonmanagers barely changed at all, dropping by a mere 1 percent from 645,000 to 638,000.

There is no question that the downsizing hit the lower levels of government the hardest. After all, that is where the pay is lowest and attrition rates the highest. The number of employees in the lower grades of the federal general employment schedule dropped by more than 170,000 between 1992 and 1997, while the number of blue-collar jobs fell by an additional 100,000. At the same time, the average employment grade of the lower-level employees who remained in the job actually increased by its largest margin in a decade, meaning that more jobs were removed at the bottom-most levels than anywhere else.

Thus, even as the bottom of government has thinned under the downsizing, the middle of government grew ever so slightly. Notwithstanding the loss of 35,000 middle-management jobs and the separation of thousands of about-to-retire employees, the average middle-level pay grade actually increased.

The relative stability in the middle-level ranks could signal the presence of one or both of two conditions. First, it could be that managers who were reclassified into nonmanagerial positions were left at the same grade. Second, it could be that most of the vacated positions were "backfilled," meaning that the occupant left, but the job and grade, sans title, were occupied by the person next in line. Neither Clinton's 1993 executive order nor the Workforce Restructuring Act required that the higher-graded jobs be forever abolished upon the incumbents' departure. The hierarchy most certainly lost weight in the total number of employees but actually gained weight as measured in the average grade of the employees who remained. This may be a diet that any overweight American would gladly follow, but it is not necessarily healthy for assuring government accountability.

It is not exactly clear where the bottom-level jobs went. Some no doubt disappeared forever; others likely ended up in service contracts. Lacking careful tracking data, one can only have suspicions. Although the Office of Management and Budget specifically asked agencies to collect information on any shift of jobs from employees to contractors, it has not monitored the data, if any data were kept at all. OMB had to depend on agencies to keep caps on contracting despite the fact that those agencies still had to deliver the same amount of goods and services. It is conceivable, for example, that many of the 300,000 jobs lost during the Clinton administration downsizing were, in fact, obsolete, but that the federal government did not have the means to eliminate them until the early 1990s. They may not have suddenly become obsolete, but they most certainly became expendable.

Finding the New Public Service

These changes clearly affected the public service, in part by introducing competition to what was once a single-sector labor market. Witness the Merit Systems Protection Board surveys of federal morale, the George Washington University surveys of Phi Beta Kappas and public administration students, and the surveys of members of Congress, presidential appointees, and senior executives.

Much as these studies have added to an understanding of what today's public servants are thinking, they do little to describe the changing nature of public service careers. One cannot know, for example, where today's public servants came from, where they went, what motivated them, and how they view their preparation for the new public service created through the changing shape of government. That kind of research would require a study of successive age cohorts, or classes, of public servants, tracking their job movements one by one over time. Ideally, such a study would have begun in the early 1970s, before the federal government began changing shape. Lacking such data, the best one can do is go back in time through the memories of respondents, tracking the contours of career job by job and describing the changing nature of public service through their choices.

Consider eight challenges in designing such a study, the first being the choice of a profession that might best reveal the changing contours of public service careers. There is certainly no shortage of professions that bear the imprint of change, from government lawyers to schoolteachers, social workers, program evaluators, environmental engineers, prison guards, rocket scientists, and computer programmers. Although each one would tell part of the story, this report focuses specifically on the professionals trained at the nation's master's-level public policy and administration programs. Not only are public policy and administration graduates the most likely to reveal the general trends described above, they represent the best of the best in the public service. If government is having trouble recruiting and holding students who have made public service the centerpiece of their graduate training, imagine the difficulties elsewhere in the recruiting process. Metaphorically, they also represent the future of the public service, a leading indicator of where jobs are moving, how careers are changing, and where government needs to get much stronger to garner its share of talented employees.

The second challenge in such a study of the new public service is to identify a specific set of public policy and administration graduates to carry this metaphorical burden. Should the study focus on a random sample of all graduates? A succession of Presidential Management Interns, which remains the federal government's premier, albeit tarnished, recruitment program for master's level graduates? Graduates who started in government but left? Those who started outside of government and recently returned? Although this report tells the story of public policy and administration graduates from every category, it focuses quite specifically on the career paths of five classes of students who attended the nation's very best programs, those rated by *U.S. News and World Report* in 1998 as the top twenty schools. Metaphorically again, these graduates should be on the leading edge of the changing public service. In theory, they should be the most heavily recruited across the sectors, and the most likely to have a choice of jobs at the start of career. To the extent that the private and nonprofit sectors are becoming more aggressive in claiming a share of the top graduates, the trend should show up first at the very top of the *U.S. News* list.

The third challenge in such a study is to choose a set of age cohorts that might provide a sense of how careers have changed over time. It is important to note that a single public opinion survey, no matter how carefully constructed to rekindle memories of first jobs, cannot substitute for a panel survey of the same respondents over time.[18] Memories change over time as current experience deconstructs and reconstructs experience. Nevertheless, without panel data, the best one can do is define a reasonable sample of respondents and discipline memory through carefully constructed questions. Toward that end, this report focuses on five separate cohorts, or classes, of public policy and administration graduates: the classes of 1973–74, 1978–79, 1983, 1988, 1993. Because respondents are more difficult to find the further back in time one goes, the first two cohorts were expanded to include two classes each to make sure that the study would have enough respondents to assure that comparisons were valid over time, while the five-year spread between classes was designed to assure reasonable distances between cohorts.

The fourth challenge in such a study using five specific classes of students is to design a fair sample that allows for careful comparison across different types of degrees. It could be, for example, that graduates of the nation's top public policy schools, which emphasize policy analysis, would head in different directions from graduates of the top public administration schools, which emphasize more traditional government-centered careers. Luckily, the *U.S. News* ratings include three types of graduate schools for such comparisons: policy analysis programs such as Carnegie Mellon and Chicago, public administration programs such as the University of Southern California and the University of Kansas, and comprehensive programs such as Harvard and Syracuse, which offer a mix of both policy and administration. Appendix A summarizes the sampling frame, type of contact information, interview procedures, and overall response rate for the survey used by Princeton Survey Research Associates to collect the data for this report in 1998 and 1999.

The fifth challenge in such a study using such a population is to collect the names and phone numbers of the actual respondents to contact. Here, the survey researcher has little choice but to rely on the kindness of the schools to provide alumni lists and the good fortune to find valid phone numbers and addresses. Unfortunately, about half of the schools in the *U.S. News* top twenty list decided not to participate in this research: Princeton (tied for number 3), California, Berkeley (tied 5), Georgia (tied 5), Duke (tied 11), Wisconsin (tied 11), American (tied 14), Columbia (tied 18), George Washington (tied 20), Rand (tied 20), Maryland (tied 20), and Pittsburgh (tied 20). Several replied that they simply did not have active alumni lists, and George Washington worried that the release of names would violate alumni confidentiality.

Luckily, the final pool of participants included representatives from all types of schools and all levels of the top twenty: Syracuse (ranked number 1), Harvard (2), Indiana (3), Texas (tied 5), Carnegie Mellon (tied 5), Michigan (tied 8), Southern California (tied 8), State University of New York, Albany (11), Chicago (tied 14), Kansas (tied 14), North Carolina (tied 14), Minnesota (tied 18), and Washington (one of five tied for 20; because of ties, there were actually twenty-four schools on the top twenty list). The final list of participants included seven comprehensive schools (Harvard, Indiana, Minnesota, North Carolina, Syracuse, Texas, and Washington), three that specialize in policy analysis (Carnegie Mellon, Chicago, and Michigan), and three that specialize in public administration (Kansas, the State University of New York at Albany, and Southern California). Most of the schools joined the study by forwarding their alumni directories, which were then scanned into a master file for final sampling. Harvard made this process all the easier by supplying an electronic version of its alumni file in several different formats.

The sixth challenge in such a study is to write a questionnaire long enough to describe changes in career but short enough to keep respondents on the line. At least for telephone surveys, where respondents always have the option of hanging up, the shorter the questionnaire, the better. Whether a survey is conducted over the telephone or in person, designing an effective questionnaire requires tough choices over both the number and range of questions. This study was no different. By keeping the number of open-ended questions to a minimum, the questionnaire was expanded to cover a wider range of issues, including career path, trust in the various sectors, the skills needed for career success, and the value of graduate education. Although open-ended questions would have yielded richer information, perhaps, the questionnaire provided a very detailed inventory of information about the past, present, and future of public service.[19] (The final survey is presented with overall percentages in appendix B.)

The seventh challenge in such a study is to actually complete the interviews. Princeton Survey Research Associates committed to making at least twenty callback attempts to connect and complete interviews with every sampled graduate (see appendix A for a brief discussion of the interview completion procedure). In all, the various alumni lists provided 3,549 telephone numbers, of which 941 were dropped because they were out of service, business, fax, or modem numbers; 184 were never answered, always busy, or somehow incomplete; 457 reached answering machines or resulted in a request to call back at another time; 474 connected to households with no eligible graduate; 477 resulted in an interview refusal; and 1,016 produced an interview. Of the interviews conducted between September 22 and November 7, 1998, only 16 produced an incomplete interview, resulting in a final sample of exactly 1,000. All told, the final response rate from the survey was 56.4 percent: 74 percent of the numbers contacted were valid; 77 percent of those numbers produced an interview; and 98 percent of those interviews were completed.

The eighth and final challenge in such a study is to analyze the data. The analyst must put the variables in the proper order, offer alternative explanations for the results, use the appropriate methodologies for separating cause from illusion, and remain cautious about interpretation and generous with possible explanations. That is very much the guiding ethic in the report that follows. This report should be taken less as *the* definitive portrait of the public service at century's end and more as a snapshot of what has happened to some of the nation's most talented public servants as they moved through career.

Plan of the Book

The rest of this book consists of four chapters, the first three offering more details on where the graduates came from, where they went, and how well they were served by their graduate education, and the fourth providing a broad overview of the findings and advice for the various actors in the new public service.

Chapter 2 starts the analysis by examining the histories that the five classes of students brought to graduate schools. Today's public policy and administration graduates are very different from their class of 1973 or 1974 predecessors. Students are more likely to bring significant work experience into school, and much of that experience is likely to occur in the private or nonprofit sector, or both. They are also likely to be more diverse demographically, as is the public service that they seek to join.

Chapter 3 continues the analysis with a profile of the new public service. The chapter starts by reviewing three decades of change in the market for public servants, and continues with a detailed examination of two defining characteristics of the new public service. First, today's public policy and administration graduates are far more likely than were their predecessors to enter the private or nonprofit sectors upon graduation, in part because both sectors have so much to offer by way of challenging work and the opportunity to grow. Second, today's graduates are also more likely to switch jobs and sectors more frequently than did their predecessors, which is no small accomplishment given the high switching rates of the earlier classes in this study. After asking why those who switch do so, the chapter concludes with an analysis of the underlying motivations to serve and the sources of job satisfaction. The new public service may be more mobile than ever, but the basic motivations to serve have remained remarkably constant over the past quarter-century: graduates of the top schools most want challenging work and the chance to grow.

Chapter 4 completes the survey analysis by asking how well the top schools served their students. The answer is both affirming and challenging. There is no doubt that the graduates interviewed for this report believe their schools gave them a degree with great value to their career success. At the same time, these graduates also report significant gaps between the skills that they believe have been important to their success and the skills that their schools taught well.

Chapter 5 concludes the report with a broad overview of findings and detailed advice to five different audiences concerned with the future of public service: students about to enroll in a public policy or administration graduate school, graduates about to enter the job market, the graduate schools themselves, government agencies that want to become more competitive in hiring talented graduates, and the non-profit sector and its funders. Presumably, the private sector already knows what it needs to do to compete.

2

PATHS INTO SERVICE

This book covers a particularly unsettled period in the history of public service. Alongside the changing shape of the federal government described in chapter 1, the government-centered public service has been through twenty-five years of sweeping reassessment of its place in civil society.[1] Always ambivalent about big government, the nation seems to agree that a smaller government is almost always a better government, even if getting smaller means that government must use a largely hidden work force of contractors and grantees to do its job. The nation also remains convinced that just about everything government touches turns to waste, creates more problems than it solves, and is mostly run for the benefit of special interests.

Not all the opinions are negative, however. Americans want more of virtually everything the federal government delivers, from aid to the poor to environmental protection, and remain mostly favorable toward government employees, particularly when they are asked about public employees, not bureaucrats, and civil servants, not politicians. Asked in 1997 whom they trusted more, Americans were five times as likely to pick civil servants who run the departments of government as to pick the politicians who lead them. Not surprisingly, perhaps, their favorable ratings of individual departments and agencies have been rising, not falling, since the mid-1980s. The U.S. Postal

Service was the public's favorite agency, with an 89 percent favorable rating, the Park Service was second at 85 percent, the Centers for Disease Control was third at 79 percent, the Defense Department was fourth at 76 percent, and the Food and Drug Administration was fifth at 75 percent.[2] Compared to the 1980s, all but a handful of agencies, including the Central Intelligence Agency and the Internal Revenue Service, gained public confidence. Little wonder, then, that the vast majority of Americans say the federal government needs only modest reform, not radical downsizing.

Despite the positives, Americans have serious doubts about how well government employees and departments are performing. Asked how well the federal government was running its programs in 1997, only a quarter of Americans answered excellent or good; half said only fair. Asked again to make a choice, they are twice as likely to say that criticism of government is justified as that government does a better job than it is given credit for.

More troubling, Americans are mostly underwhelmed with the federal government's actual performance in delivering the goods and services they want. Asked about the federal government's success in achieving eight specific goals—from setting academic standards for schools to conserving natural resources—a majority of Americans give government excellent or good marks on only one, ensuring that foods and medicines are safe (58 percent). The seven other goals fall far below, with 85 percent of the public rating the government's job in reducing juvenile delinquency only fair or poor.

These ratings are particularly interesting when compared to the ratings of departments and agencies discussed above. Three-quarters of Americans may have given the Food and Drug Administration a favorable rating, but only 58 percent said the federal government is doing an excellent or good job of ensuring that food and medicines are safe; 69 percent may have given the Environmental Protection Agency a favorable mark, but only 34 percent said the federal government is doing an excellent or good job of conserving the country's natural resources. The performance gaps continue all the way down the list to the Department of Education, which earned a 61 percent favorable rating as an institution, but a 23 percent excellent or good rating in setting academic standards for the schools and just 18 percent on ensuring that all Americans can afford to send their children to college.

When the positives and negatives are pulled together, a simple portrait emerges. Americans want the public service to do the impossible. As public administration scholar Charles Goodsell puts it, they give the public service "inconsistent, contradictory, and hence unachievable goals and tasks," demand that it "achieve results indirectly, through the efforts of others," evaluate it "not by how much it *tries* to move ahead on an impossible front but by whether or not 'success' is achieved," and both oversell and undersell what it does.[3] Instead of wanting a government that "works better and costs less," which was the early mantra of Vice President Al Gore's reinventing government campaign, the polling data suggest that Americans want a government that looks smaller and delivers at least as much. With government workers under unrelenting pressure to deliver the goods, yet under constant attack from the public, the media, and often their own leaders, it would not be surprising to find that graduates of the top public policy and administration schools might be asking whether they took the right path in entering public service in the first place.

The First to Enter

The classes of 1973 and 1974 offer a nearly perfect opportunity to examine the changing context of public service over the past quarter-century. They could not have picked a more turbulent moment to enter public service, whether measured by political, bureaucratic, reform, civil service, or cultural time.

Start with political time, where the classes of 1973 and 1974 entered service at the end of one potential impeachment and celebrated their twenty-fifth reunions in the midst of an actual one. Completing their programs just as the Watergate scandal peaked, they watched as the number of Americans who trust the government in Washington to do the right thing just about always or most of the time continued its long tumble. Having hit a fifty-year peak at 74 percent in the mid-1960s, trust fell from 36 percent in 1974 to its fifty-year low of just 21 percent in 1994. But for one short-lived rise just before the Iran-contra arms-for-hostages scandal broke in the late 1980s, and another just before President Clinton ensnared himself in a year-long sex scandal in 1998, the tumble never abated. Despite a respite here and there, most notably in the "good-people-trapped-in-bad-systems" rhetoric that has marked Gore's reinventing campaign, the classes of 1973 and 1974 have been the subject more of derision and attack from their own leaders than of respect and celebration.

The classes of 1973 and 1974 had to be part of the cynicism, too. Bathed in the Vietnam War and Watergate, they carried the markers of a generation that struck an independent course. By 1965, political scientists M. Kent Jennings and Richard Niemi had already detected the first evidence of a breakdown in the traditional political socialization process between the parents of the baby boom and their children. In the first of what would be three waves of interviews with the parents and children, Jennings and Niemi found one low statistical correlation after another in comparing attitudes within the same families. Even in the third of the cases where the parents and students agreed on party identification, Jennings and Niemi worried about the lack of cross-generational embrace. The most they could say about the success of the parents in teaching their children about politics was "that there is considerable slack in the value-acquisition process."[4]

Interviewing the parents and children a second time in 1973 (about the time that some of those children would have been in public policy and administration graduate school), the University of Michigan scholars found that even the party agreements had eroded. In a harbinger of future career patterns, perhaps, roughly 40 percent of the children changed their basic party identification (Democrat, Republican, or independent) between 1965 and 1973. Adding in intensity (strong, weak, or leaning), almost 70 percent had changed. Only a quarter of the children who had been strong Democrats in 1965 were still strong Democrats in 1973—most had become weak Democrats or independent-leaning Democrats. And only a third of the children who had been strong Republicans in the mid-1960s were still strong Republicans eight years later. It is important to note that the parents mostly stayed put. The children were shaking free of their party attachments on their own, embracing a conditional loyalty of a sort built around a retrospective assessment of party performance at election time.[5]

Continue with bureaucratic time, where the classes of 1973 and 1974 entered service at the start of a twenty-five year-war on waste. Having accepted their diplomas as Congress finished its sweeping investigation of welfare fraud and created the first statutory inspector general to root out wrongdoing from the inside of government, they watched as the "visible odium of deterrence" infused every corner of the federal bureaucracy and began to percolate ever downward into the states and localities and the nonprofit sector. By 1998 there would be inspectors general in fifty-seven departments and agencies, twenty-seven appointed by the president and confirmed by the Senate and thirty appointed by the agency head without further review. Not surprisingly, the result was a steady increase in the amount of fraud, waste, and abuse discovered in government, at least as measured by the yearly records in the statistical inventory of investigations opened, dollars recovered, and funds put to better use, whatever that term meant.[6]

None of this is to argue that the inspectors general made the government-centered service less attractive, for there is no doubt that some agencies became more effective as a result of tightened compliance and greater scrutiny. At the same time, however, there is no question that the war on waste put government employees under the scrutiny of a growing corps of inspectors, auditors, and investigators. As Ronald Reagan argued in his first inaugural, "government is not the solution to our problem; government is the problem. . . . It is time to check and reverse the growth of government, which shows signs of having grown beyond the consent of the governed." Much as Gore resisted such broad strokes, the introduction to his first reinventing report repeats the same war-on-waste refrain: "The federal government seems unable to abandon the obsolete. It knows how to add, but not to subtract. And yet, waste is not the only problem. The federal government is not simply broke; it is broken." The parallels were more than rhetorical. The Reagan administration began with an immediate hiring freeze, while the Clinton administration began with an executive order mandating a 100,000 cut in the total federal work force.[7]

Turn next to reform time, where the classes of 1973 and 1974 left their graduate programs at the beginning of a long-term acceleration in all four tides of reform that have shaped the way government delivers its goods and services over the past half-century. Much of the acceleration involved an increase in congressional activism following Watergate. Not only did Congress intensify the war on waste through eighteen amendments to the Federal Inspector General Act between 1978 and 1998, it also expanded its long-standing efforts to open government to the sunshine through amendments to statutes such as Freedom of Information and Administrative Procedures.

Because the presidency continued to produce its own reforms over the years, albeit more through executive orders and administrative reforms such as hiring ceilings (war on waste) and reinventing campaigns (liberation management) than legislation, the result was a cacophony of reform. "Congress and the president appear to be less patient," I wrote in 1997, "reforming past reforms more frequently and shifting direction more quickly. The more government is reformed, the more Congress and the president think it needs further reforming."[8] With ninety-three major reform statutes passed since their graduations in 1974, it is safe to say that the classes of 1973 and 1974 have seen more bureaucratic change in their first quarter-century of service than any comparable cohort in history. It is also safe to predict that every successive class studied for this report will see even more, as Congress and the president move from management by objectives to performance-based budgeting and back, competition in contracting to acquisition streamlining and back, pay for performance to broad banding and back, quality management to reengineering and back, all coupled with the standard pay freezes, employment ceilings, and constant pressure to privatize and outsource.[9]

Turn next to civil service time, where the classes of 1973 and 1974 have mostly watched time stand still inside government, even as the rest of the economy has been awakening to the emergence of a lasting labor shortage. Indeed, just about every sector *but* government seems to realize that talent is scarce. According to a recent study published in the *McKinsey Quarterly,* search firm revenues grew twice as fast as gross domestic product between 1993 and 1998. The growth can only increase as the huge baby boom edges toward retirement and the number of 35 to 44 year-olds declines by a sixth over the next fifteen years. Together, the trends create a steadily dwindling pool of executives that cannot be offset by increased productivity or longer careers among existing cohorts of executives.[10]

And how well did the federal government respond to this challenge? The answers are mixed at best. The good news is that federal benefits have more than kept pace with the private sector, at last review in 1998 ranging from 26 percent to 50 percent of federal pay compared to 24 percent to 44 percent of pay for large private firms.[11] According to the U.S. Congressional Budget Office, federal vacation, holiday, retirement (specifically the Federal Employee Retirement System, FERS), disability, and retiree health benefits are generally more generous than private equivalents, while federal health and life insurance lag behind.

The bad news is that federal pay has not kept pace. As of 1997 the average pay gap between comparable federal and private jobs was 22 percent, with the greatest distance coming in the more highly skilled professional, administrative, and technical positions—in short, the positions that are most likely to be the focus of private sector competition. Because federal pay and benefits combined would "still be well below what large firms offer for similar jobs—even for federal employees with the largest relative advantage in the value of benefits," CBO concludes, "for some jobs, the government has to accept employees with less experience and education than do private firms recruiting for many of the same types of jobs." Turns out that it is even better to be downsized by a private contractor to the federal government than by government itself. Private contractors to the Department of Energy are allowed to provide larger voluntary buyouts for their employees than the department provides to its own—federal buyout incentives are capped at $25,000 maximum, whereas private contractors can negotiate their own agreements.[12]

The pay gap clearly affects the long-term health of the federal service. Asked what might make a difference in recruiting and retaining government talent, a 1999 PricewaterhouseCoopers survey ranked competitive pay and compensation as simultaneously the most helpful and least likely solution among a sample of senior executives drawn from across government. Whereas 72 percent of the 347 senior executives said higher compensation would make government more competitive, only 5 percent thought Congress and the president would actually act to implement reform. As if to confirm the difficulty of finding a useful reform that can pass political muster, the senior executives also rated the most likely reform, developing staff through training and the senior executive development program, as among the least helpful.[13] (Apropos of the changing shape of government, the PricewaterhouseCoopers survey was released on the same day that the Washington Post reported a proposed Defense Department initiative to convert as many as 400,000 uniformed military jobs to contractor positions, including thousands of battlefield support jobs that would put the contractors in harm's way.)[14]

Pay and benefits are obviously only part of the personnel problem, however. The classes of 1973 and 1974 also entered service as the civil service began the long, ill-planned fragmentation discussed in chapter 1. Would that every scholar were as prescient as Charles H. Levine and Rosslyn S. Kleeman in making the following prediction in 1986: "If present trends continue, there is a substantial chance that the civil service system will break up into what amounts to a dual structure. To say this is to assume that the stalemate over a comprehensive civil service policy will continue and that Congress and the president will reform small pieces of the system one at a time. Under such a process, the civil service system seems likely to break into two parts, the haves and the have-nots, gradually fraying first the edges and then the core of the present system."[15]

Parts of their prediction, most notably the outsourcing fever, came to pass with surprising intensity, while others, most notably the breakaway of scientists, engineers, lawyers, and other specialty occupations from the confines of the traditional civil service, have been slower to take hold. Nevertheless, Levine and Kleeman were quite right to warn that the system was drifting toward mediocrity as government pay trailed the private sector, and good jobs leached through an increasingly porous boundary between government and the private and nonprofit sectors. Coupled with the shift from a baby-boom labor surplus to a Generation X labor shortage, government has never been under greater pressure to compete for talent, yet arguably never less prepared.

Turn last to cultural time, where the classes of 1973 and 1974 finished their degrees in the midst of what appears to have been a broad separation from work. As the first baby boomers to graduate from the top public policy and administration schools, they were clearly energized by the promise of the New Frontier and the Great Society. At the same time, the classes of 1973 and 1974 were on the leading edge of a broad abandonment of traditional social and institutional ties. Working from detailed surveys of social meaning in 1957 and 1976, social psychologists Joseph Veroff, Elizabeth Douvan, and Richard Kulka found undeniable evidence that Americans of all ages had pulled back from traditional social structures. Respondents were much less willing to talk about what they did for a living in 1976 than they were in 1957, for example, prompting Veroff and his colleagues to muse about the potential psychological loss embedded in the anonymity. "Knowing what a person does can reveal a good deal of information about the personal organization, the essential and authentic aspects of a person. . . . What a person does is related to what he [or she] is—in his [or her] core."[16]

The surveys also showed a sharp decline in the use of traditional social labels to mark oneself, be it party identification, job title, or social groups. The classes of 1973 and 1974 were part of a generation that preferred to be known on a first-name basis. The paradox, according to Veroff and his colleagues, is "that disregard for status, which is urged as a counterthrust to formalism and status conscious-ness out of a desire to reduce obstacles to close interaction between people, actually *increases* distance between people by insisting that they turn inward for the derivation of meaning and self-definition, by placing the burden of self-definition entirely on the individual—and making it a matter of individual achievement rather than a consensual and shared reality."

Veroff and his colleagues also found growing evidence of a separa-tion from the traditional meanings of work. "Suits and ties may have replaced blue jeans and t-shirts," I wrote in reviewing the data in the mid-1980s, "but the baby boomers appear to retain much of their commitment to finding a meaningful philosophy of life, even in the workplace. Baby boomers tend to value the content of work more than their parents, and appear to look for satisfaction and challenge to a somewhat greater extent." Work also declined as a source of psycho-logical meaning. In 1955, for example, a sample of Americans under the age of thirty (many of whom were parents of baby boomers) agreed in a Gallup poll that they sometimes enjoyed their work so much that they had trouble putting it aside at the end of the day. By 1980 only a quarter of another sample of Americans under the age of thirty (now the baby boomers themselves) agreed with the statement, even though their parents remained just as committed to work.[17]

When the vicissitudes of political, bureaucratic, reform, civil ser-vice, and cultural time are viewed in their entirety, it would be shock-ing if they did not affect the public service. After all, the public service is never just a passive target of change. It is also a source of change in itself, whether in workplace reforms such as flextime and parental leave that it advocates and implements, or in the adjustments its own members make to the evolving culture. As its members change with the times, so do their professions.

Moreover, the changes described above did not occur in a public service vacuum. They were refracted through massive demographic, economic, and technological change, including the aging of the work force, the globalization of the economy, and the exponential gains in computing speed. Given all that has happened over the past quarter-century, it is nearly impossible to create a scenario under which the government-centered public service could have survived intact. As the next chapter will show, the result has been a steady erosion of the old public service as the paths into service and destinations of career have reshaped the profile of the profession.

Before turning to the inventory of change, it is important to note the one constant over time. As the next chapter will show, the five classes may have come from different places and gone on to different careers, but they nonetheless share a common commitment to making a difference in the world around them. In a sense, the commitment to public service will out, whether in private firms that now do the work once done inside government, in the small nonprofits that survive month to month in an increasingly competitive environment, or in government agencies that have been through a quarter-century of nearly ceaseless reinventing. If there is one finding worth heralding and repeating, it is that the public service ethic remains as engaging today as it was twenty-five years ago. It may be under duress, but it is most certainly alive.

The Histories They Brought

Future public servants bring more than time and tuition to graduate school. They also bring their personal, intellectual, and work histories, not the least of which involves the public service experience they may have had between college and graduate school. The days when college and graduate school involved an unbroken five- or six-year march from a bachelor's degree to master's are long gone, pushed aside partly by undergraduate debt, rising graduate school tuition, and a growing reluctance among public policy and administration schools' admission committees to accept students without at least some experience.

There can be little doubt that the paths into service, at least as measured by graduates of the nation's top public policy and administration master's programs, have changed dramatically over the past quarter-century. Extrapolating from the survey that forms the basis of this report, today's graduating class is more diverse demographically, more moderate ideologically, more Democratic politically, more likely to bring significant work experience into graduate school, and more interested in the private and nonprofit sectors as potential employers than was any cohort in recent history. Although some of the trends reflect life-cycle effects—that is, the cumulative impact of aging—the top graduate programs are dealing with a very different kind of student from the ones who enrolled the classes of 1973 and 1974. So, too, is government.

Demographic Histories

The nation's top public policy and administration graduate schools have made remarkable progress in building a more diverse student body over the past quarter century, particularly by increasing access for women. As figure 2-1 shows, the number of women has moved steadily upward from just 22 percent in the classes of 1973 and 1974 to 37 percent in 1978–79, 40 percent in 1983, 46 percent in 1988, and 52 percent in 1993. Rarely do researchers see such a straight line. Following the 15 percent jump in the mid-1970s, a jump that appears to be linked to a desire or need for more work experience before entering graduate school among women in the early classes, the gender diversity rises by almost equal amounts class to class thereafter.

The increasing gender diversity creates a tangle of explanations for the rise of the multisector public service. Although men and women in more recent classes are almost equally likely to have worked before entering graduate school, women were far more likely to have earned their experience in the nonprofit sector (32 percent of women versus 16 percent of men), and far less likely to have worked in government (39 percent of women versus 54 percent of men). This is not to argue that nonprofits are exclusively of interest to women students. Women graduates were only slightly less likely to turn to government for their first postgraduate jobs than were men, and only slightly more likely to go nonprofit.

Moreover, there is no evidence to suggest that the women graduates were motivated by a different set of goals in pursuing public service. The genders were virtually indistinguishable in their basic desire for

Figure 2-1. Demographic Diversity, by Class[a]

Percent of class

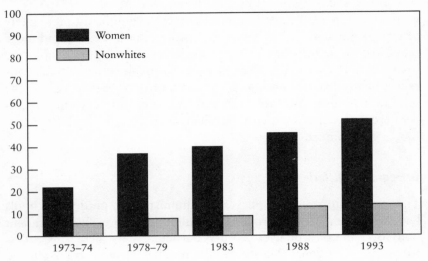

a. N = 200 for 1973–74; N = 231 for 1978–79; N = 171 for 1983; N = 192 for 1988; N = 196 for 1993.

challenging work, opportunity for personal growth and skill development, opportunity for advancement, benefits, security, and pay. They were also virtually indistinguishable in their assessment of the quality of their graduate training, and in their assessment of the skills that have been most important to their career success (maintaining ethical standards is the top skill reported by women and men alike). In short, women may be much more likely to enter graduate school with non-profit experience, and somewhat more likely to leave graduate school for nonprofit destinations, but they seek the same skills as men, regardless of their eventual career destination. As such, the increasing gender diversity of America's top public policy and administration graduate schools shows the power of simply opening the doors to women.

The schools have also done well in opening the doors to students of color, moving up steadily over the years in large part because of a twenty-year investment by the Sloan and Ford Foundations in preparing minority college students for graduate study in public policy and administration. As figure 2-2 shows, only 6 percent of the classes of

Figure 2-2. Very Important Considerations for First Job, by Race[a]

Percent very important

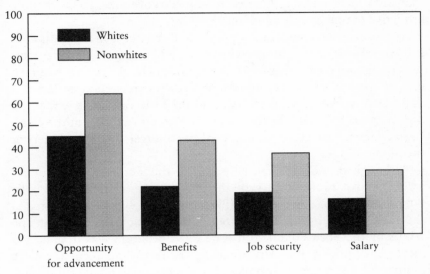

a. N = 849 for whites; N = 91 for nonwhites.

1973 and 1974 identified themselves as nonwhites, compared to 14 percent in the class of 1993. Although the 1993 number is still low overall when compared to the expected demand for nonwhite workers in the coming decades, it does reflect gains in every racial group. The percentage of African Americans rose from 4 to 6 percent; the number of Asian Americans from 2 to 4 percent; the number of Hispanics or Latinos from 2 to 7 percent.

As racial diversity increased, so did the diversity of work experience. Although whites and nonwhites were equally likely to have worked before entering graduate school, nonwhites worked more years before returning and were significantly more likely to have worked in the private sector. Nonwhites were also more likely than were whites to move into government immediately after graduation, and far less likely to pick nonprofits as a career destination. Subsample sizes being relatively small, one can only speculate on the lack of interest in nonprofits. However, there is no question that benefits, job security, and salary weighed more heavily on the minds of nonwhite students than of whites in picking their first jobs, suggesting, if not proving, that nonwhites may have entered school with much more significant financial burdens than did whites, burdens that may have made government a much more attractive option after graduation.

Where racial diversity did not make a difference is in the skills considered very important for career success, with one notable difference: by a margin of 67 percent to 41 percent, nonwhites rated managing a diverse work force as very important to their career success. The fact that they saw the demand as critical to their success, while whites did not, suggests a potential gap in what whites are learning in the classroom, particularly given the expected rise in diversity in all corners of the public sector.

Although the schools can be proud of the increased diversity described above, much of the growth appears to be related to the Public Policy and International Affairs (PPIA) program, which was started in the early 1980s by the Sloan Foundation and carried through the 1990s by the Ford Foundation. The PPIA program was designed to increase the pool of minority applicants by recruiting talented college juniors for a summer skill-building institute at one of six public policy and administration graduate schools.

No one can know whether the top schools would have become more diverse without the 2,000 PPIA alumni, who formed a potential recruiting pool for the future. After all, the schools were under great pressure to change. What is clear, however, is that the PPIA program produced roughly 150 alumni each year, thereby significantly increasing the odds that the schools could find students of color who were ready and motivated to apply. (The history of the PPIA program can be found in *Our Story*, a summary of the program's twenty-year history.)[18]

That the program succeeded in preparing students of color for the public service is clear in the available data on its graduates. First, by preparing students of color to attend the nation's leading public policy and administration graduate schools, the PPIA program clearly expanded the pool of professionals of color who enter the public service in both international affairs and domestic policy. The program has done so by admitting a mix of students to the summer institutes, maintaining a demographic and intellectual balance among its participants.[19] Some students arrive already having taken the basic courses in quantitative methods and policy analysis needed for graduate success, whereas others arrive with little or no exposure to those topics.

But both find ample opportunity to learn. Although it is impossible to know what percentage of the PPIA participants would have entered graduate school without the experience, there is no doubt from the evaluations that the summer institutes raise the basic skill levels of all students who attend, regardless of where they start in their familiarity with the core disciplines.

Second, there is compelling evidence that the summer institutes provide needed grounding in economics, statistics, and policy analysis. Although there appears to be room for more exposure to international policy, PPIA students are generally receiving broad contact with both domestic and international issues and topics. Overall, the consensus is that the program provides substantial value added for students who participate. An evaluation of the Fellows who entered the program from 1989 to 1992 by the Joint Center for Political and Economic Studies also suggests that the program increased student interest in public service careers, including significant gains in interest in international affairs after both the junior and senior summer institutes.[20]

Third, the PPIA program makes a substantial contribution to student success through its links to the world of practice. Indeed, networking was mentioned by the 1989–92 students as the single most important benefit of the summer institutes. Students who attend one of the five summer institutes develop strong bonds with each other, building friendships that last through graduate school and beyond. Many of these contacts mature into enduring professional relationships and mentoring opportunities for the students involved. In addition, field visits to public, nonprofit, and international organizations have added substantially to student understanding of public policy.

Fourth, most of the individuals who attend the summer institutes eventually matriculate at one of the thirty-seven participating graduate schools, and most graduate to careers in public service. Roughly 75 percent of the PPIA summer participants entered graduate school in public policy or international affairs; nearly all of them entered a master's degree program, and some of them showed up in the sample for the present study.

Finally, a majority of the participants find their way into careers in public policy and administration. With the class of 1989, which would have been the most likely to have found employment by the time the Joint Center for Political Studies began its comprehensive evaluation, almost half were employed in federal, state, or local government, and another third in the nonprofit sector. Among students who were either unemployed or not working in public service, interest in moving to the public service remained high.

Despite its success, the PPIA program is being phased out as this book goes to press. The Ford Foundation has decided to invest its resources in a broader effort to support the next generation of urban leaders, and no other foundation stands ready to take over. At some point, the philanthropic community is right to ask when the schools of public policy and administration, not to mention the end-consumers of their students, will absorb the costs of recruiting students of color on their own. Unless they answer quickly, the top schools will be hard pressed to maintain the gains in racial diversity documented here.

Intellectual Histories

One of the great challenges in public policy and administration education is the lack of a common undergraduate history among future professionals. The students at the top schools come from every possible background, drawn to graduate school in part by a commitment to public service, and in part perhaps by a rejection of other graduate options such as law and business. If undergraduate major is any indication of intellectual diversity, the top schools are drawing a very diverse student body indeed.[21] As for the dominance of any major, there is none. Broken down into individual majors in table 2-1, political science accounts for one in four graduates total, with a choppy decline from 35 percent in the classes of 1973–74 to 25 percent in the class of 1993; while history accounts for one in twelve, also with a slight decline; and economics accounts for one in sixteen, with a slight increase over time.

This is not to discount modest variations in program preferences by undergraduate major, however. Business, political science, psychology, sociology, and, not at all surprisingly, public administration majors were more likely to attend the public administration programs covered by the survey (Kansas, SUNY Albany, and Southern California) than the policy analysis (Carnegie Mellon, Chicago, and Michigan) or comprehensive programs (Harvard, Indiana, Minnesota, North Carolina, Syracuse, Texas, and Washington); accounting, economics, international relations, and journalism majors were more likely to attend comprehensive programs than either policy analysis or public admin-

Table 2-1. Intellectual Histories, by Class[a]

Percent

Undergraduate major	Class				
	1973–74	1978–79	1983	1988	1993
Business	8	5	4	11	8
Humanities	21	27	23	23	22
Political science	35	26	37	29	25
Hard sciences	16	13	9	17	14
Social sciences	18	22	26	17	27

a. N = 200 for 1973–74; N = 231 for 1978–79; N = 171 for 1983; N = 192 for 1988; N = 196 for 1993.

istration; and public health majors showed a slight preference for policy analysis over comprehensive and public administration. It is difficult to ascribe much deliberation to the movement, however, particularly since the top public administration programs have historically enrolled more students than the comprehensive and public policy schools, and account for two-and-a-half times as many respondents in the sample discussed here. Nevertheless, at least some of the sorting may reflect perceptions of the relative emphasis given to quantitative methods and microanalysis at the public policy schools, perceptions that may drive the humanistic majors toward public administration or comprehensive programs.

Woe be to any school that focuses just on one major, however. Even public administration programs, which drew a fifth of their students from public administration (7 percent) and political science (13 percent) combined and tend to focus on government as a primary focus of their teaching, must reach out to nontraditional majors to fill their rolls: 3 percent from communications, 4 percent came from math, 4 percent from foreign languages, 4 percent from engineering, 4 percent from English, 4 percent from economics, and 4 percent from the sciences broadly defined, 6 percent from psychology, 7 percent from business, and 10 percent from history. As for the more mathematically oriented policy analysis programs, 3 percent of their students came from psychology, 3 percent from journalism, 6 percent from English, and 8 percent from history. It is far better for the programs to consider themselves blessed by the remarkable range of undergraduate interest that greets them each year, even if it is virtually impossible to tailor a program for any specific major.

As chapter 4 will show, the lack of a common intellectual background affects the core curricula of the top programs. Suffice it to note here that all of the schools spend an inordinate amount of time in what can only be described as remedial education in microeconomics and quantitative methods. With the more humanistic majors representing nearly a quarter of all students (1 percent anthropology, 1 percent philosophy, 1 percent social studies, 2 percent journalism, 2 percent education, 2 percent communications, 3 percent foreign languages, 3 percent sociology, and 9 percent history), it is not clear that the programs have a choice. The schools must build the profession mostly from scratch, adding common skills and languages to what the students bring with them in intellectual ability.

As with gender and race, intellectual diversity did not have a significant impact on where the graduates went. Although political science majors were half again as likely to enter government for their first jobs out of graduate school than any other majors (61 percent versus 44 percent for all of the other majors combined), they also accounted for nearly a third of all those who later switched from government to the private or nonprofit sectors. It is not that political science majors were dramatically less loyal to their first employers, however. Political science majors were just as likely to stay in the sector where they started (58 percent) as humanities (63 percent), sciences (61 percent), and social science (58 percent) majors. Rather, as we shall see later, it is that graduates who took their first jobs in government were less likely to stay put than were graduates who took their first jobs outside of government. And although 74 percent of business majors were more likely to stay put in the sector where they started, they were no more likely than were any other graduates to start their careers in the private sector or to move to the sector later in career.

Wherever they may have started, the majors shared similar hopes for their first jobs, suggesting again a shared set of public service expectations among all students entering the profession. At the top of the list of important considerations, business majors were somewhat more likely than other majors to emphasize the opportunity to do challenging work, while social science majors were less concerned with the type of work they would be doing. Business majors also were more likely to emphasize benefits and job security.

But that is where the differences end. All of the majors shared a common desire for personal growth and skill advancement; all shared a concern for public respect; and few shared much concern for salary. Even these few differences tended to smooth out as the graduates have progressed through their careers. Business majors cooled down a bit on the desire for challenging work in moving from first to current jobs (down from 89 percent in first jobs to 75 percent in current), while social science majors became a bit hotter about the type of work (up from 63 percent in first jobs to 71 percent in current), but life worked its will in smoothing the edges of career. Having left graduate school mostly in agreement about career goals, members of the profession moved further from their disciplinary roots and more toward a common desire for challenging work and the opportunity to grow. Life worked its will on concerns for tangible benefits, too, where the profession become more and more concerned about benefits, salary, and security. (Readers are forewarned that there *are* significant differences in career goals, however, if not by gender, race, and undergraduate major, then most certainly by the sector where they work.)

Work Histories

Students arrive at graduate school with an assortment of experiences that shape their readiness to learn. Some of those experiences involve gender and race, others the intellectual training they received as undergraduates. Although public policy and administration schools have always drawn a majority of their students from the ranks of the working, the past three decades have witnessed not only a significant increase in the work experience of entering students, but a dramatic change in where that experience has taken place.

More recent classes were not only less likely to come directly to graduate school, they were much more likely to come with more than five years of experience. Removing mid-career students from the sample reduces the overall number of highly experienced students, but not the sharpness of the trend. Today's students are arriving at the graduate school door with much greater experience than in the past, in part because schools such as Syracuse University's Maxwell School are focusing more on mid-career students, and in part no doubt because the students themselves are taking time to relieve some of their undergraduate debt. This trend is evident in figure 2-3.

More important to the career destinations discussed later, younger classes earned their experience in very different places from their baby

Figure 2-3. Work Experience, by Class[a]

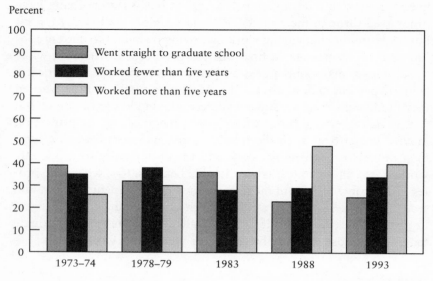

Percent

a. $N = 200$ for 1973–74; $N = 231$ for 1978–79; $N = 171$ for 1983; $N = 192$ for 1988; $N = 196$ for 1993.

boomer peers. Whereas government accounted for 73 percent of the work experience in the classes of 1973–74, it provided 46 percent of the experience in the class of 1988 and just 35 percent of the class of 1993. And whereas the nonprofit sector accounted for just 12 percent of the experience in the classes of 1973–74, it produced 25 percent of the experience in the class of 1988 and 31 percent in the class of 1993. The private sector was relatively steady over all of the classes, rising ever so slightly over time.

When analyzed in total, roughly one-third of the classes of 1973–74 and 1978–79 entered graduate school directly from college, another third from government, and the final third from the private and nonprofit sectors, while roughly one-quarter of the classes of 1988 and 1993 entered directly from college, slightly less than a third from government, and almost two out of five from the private and nonprofit sectors. The trend holds even when Harvard and Syracuse and their large number of mid-career students are removed from the sample.

These work histories clearly create a presumption in the career destinations discussed below. Spending time in government, private firms, or nonprofit agencies before entering graduate school increases the odds of a return afterwards. Students who worked in government before entering graduate school were more than twice as likely to be in government when they were interviewed for this study than were students who entered graduate school after working in nonprofit agencies. Conversely, students who worked in the nonprofit sector before entering graduate school were nearly three times as likely to be back in the nonprofit sector than were students who had worked in government before graduate school. Interestingly, those who came to graduate school with private sector experience were only slightly more likely to be found back in their sector than in government or nonprofit agencies.

The commitment to returning to the nonprofit sector is particularly noticeable among recent classes, suggesting a growing commitment to going nonprofit among today's students. Among the nonprofit veterans who entered the classes of 1973 and 1974, for example, only 27 percent are still there today; among their peers in the class of 1988, the number is 53 percent. It is just too early to judge where the class of 1993 will end up, since so many are still in their first jobs, but the early indications are that the nonprofit sector will be just as sticky for them.

As with the other data presented above, work history does not shape the basic motivations of service among public policy and administration graduates. Once again, there is striking evidence of the core desires among all public service professionals, regardless of where they came from. Except for a significantly lower interest in opportunities to impact local or national issues among private sector veterans and a significantly higher desire for public respect among nonprofit veterans, there is virtually no statistical difference at the top of the list of very important considerations in taking first jobs. Further down the list, however, nonprofit veterans express less concern for benefits and job security, perhaps suggesting early socialization about the high level of benefits of public service from their experiences working in cash-strapped, relatively insecure nonprofit agencies. These differences disappear with the passage of career into the present, however. Even those with private sector experience come to recognize the value of public respect, for example, while those with nonprofit experience eventually come to grips with the value of benefits and security.

Political and Ideological Histories

Because of time limits in the survey, there is little to be said here of the political and ideological histories that the graduates brought with them. If there are hints of the past in the present, and political socialization theory would say that the past is very much a predictor of the present and future, the general profile of the public policy and administration graduates could be easily described as Democratic and moderate or center-left. Overall, 36 percent of the sample described itself as either very liberal or liberal, another 47 percent as moderate, and only 19 percent as conservative. Although there were slight differences over the five classes, with the older classes being slightly more conservative than the class of 1993, the differences are negligible statistically and track trends in the public at large.

Where the classes divide is on party identification. By a margin of 43 percent to 28 percent, members of the classes of 1973 and 1974 were much more likely than the class of 1993 to identify themselves as political independents than were the younger classes, suggesting the enduring effects of having coming of age politically during the Vietnam and Watergate era. It is a period effect that wore off relatively quickly, however, leaving no noticeable mark even on the classes of 1978 and 1979 five years later. It is also a period effect that is confirmed in national data from the time. The increase in the number of independents was limited to the early 1970s.

Moreover, it is an effect that has virtually no impact on any of the trends in career to be discussed in the next section. Of the few significant differences between parties, for example, the most logical comes far down on the list of very important considerations in taking current jobs. There, exactly half of Republicans rank salary as a very important consideration, compared to just a third of Democrats. But other than that basic motivational conflict, party identifiers and independents alike share that core commitment to finding challenging work (77 percent for Republicans, 78 percent for Democrats, and 76 percent for independents), opportunity for personal growth (68 percent, 75 percent, and 74 percent), type of work (65 percent, 74 percent, and 72 percent), and opportunity to impact local and national issues (52 percent, 56 percent, and 52 percent) that marks the profession across the histories described above.

Conclusion

Lost in all the data on paths into service is the remarkable diversity of the graduates interviewed for this study. The nation's public policy and administration schools have become increasingly attractive to what were once considered nontraditional students. Facing increased competition from business schools, which have been launching nonprofit programs in record numbers, the public policy and administration schools have kept the barriers to entry low, while providing the evening and mid-career programs that would attract an increasingly experienced clientele. At the same time, they have created an educational climate that appears to be increasingly attractive to women and students of color, albeit a climate that can always tolerate further improvement. The exception has become the norm.

There is a cost, of course, to the welcoming. Because they have mostly refused to require microeconomics and quantitative methods as prerequisites for admission, for example, the schools must devote extraordinary time to teaching their English majors, historians, and other humanists the basics. Unfortunately, because they have mostly refused to require American government or international relations as prerequisites, but because they can only do so much catching up in the core curriculum, they must rely on their economists, physicists, and other hard majors to learn more about how the democratic process works on their own. Finally, because there are so few opportunities for students to teach each other, much of the diversity goes to waste. Students enter with a wide range of experiences but tend to receive a fairly fixed set of core skills. As chapter 4 will argue, the schools may not have kept pace with the increased diversity. Much as they should be applauded for opening the doors to diversity, and much as these graduates believe that their education has served them well, the top schools still have room to grow in providing the learning opportunities that their rapidly changing student body deserves.

3

A PROFILE OF THE PROFESSION

The end of the government-centered public service was hardly caused by the nation's top public policy and administration schools. Would that they were so powerful. Rather, it was caused in part by the rising tide of public cynicism, the wave upon wave of administrative reform, the thickening of federal hierarchy, the sluggishness of the hiring process, and the acceleration in outsourcing.

The end of the government-centered public service was not just a reaction to the onslaught of negatives, however. It also involved attractive new opportunities in both the private and nonprofit sectors, whether to pay down debts and learn new skills or to make a visible difference on issues that matter. As government became less competitive as a destination of career, as well as a less prominent recruiting presence on college campuses, both the private and nonprofit sectors became more noticeable. Private firms began showing up at the top schools with their bundles of cash in October of the final year, while the nonprofit sector was never far from sight for students who had already set records for volunteering as undergraduates.

The end of the government-centered public service does not mean that the top public policy and administration schools have failed somehow. To the contrary, there is ample evidence in the following pages that they have succeeded, if sometimes by accident, in preparing their graduates for the multisectored careers that government itself has forged through outsourcing and devolution. Their graduates are still answering the call to public service. It is just no longer coming exclusively or even predominantly from government. It is a combination of change and stability that can be seen in both the destinations of career and the motivation to serve, which are the two main concerns of this chapter.

The Destinations of Career

Having arrived in graduate school from a wide range of starting points, the professionals interviewed for this report left with a common set of understandings regarding public policy and administration, not the least of which was a grounding in the core methods of policy analysis. Although there are significant differences between what public policy and public administration schools teach, the top twenty schools have mostly agreed that microeconomics and quantitative methods are the central tools of the profession. As the next chapter will show, the schools devote more than half of their core curriculums to the two topics. Not surprisingly, their students recognize the emphasis. Policy analysis was ranked as the number one skill that these graduates thought their schools taught well.

Despite their shared core curricula and common commitment to making a difference, the five classes interviewed for this report have become steadily less interested in government as a destination for service. Table 3-1 makes the empirical case. First, the number of graduates who started out in government declined from a high of 76 percent in the classes of 1973 and 1974 to just 49 percent in 1993. Of the 76 percent who went into government, 28 percent went into federal jobs, 30 percent went into state jobs, and 30 percent went into local jobs, a distribution pattern that had not changed by 1993. Because a smaller proportion of the class of 1993 went into government, however, the federal, state, and local share of the talent pool fell sharply. When all the numbers are totaled up, 21 percent of the classes of 1973/74 took first jobs in the federal government, compared to just 15 percent of the class of 1993.

Second, the number of graduates who were working in government at the time of this survey declined from 50 percent among the classes of 1973 and 1974 to 41 percent in the class of 1993. The figures

Table 3-1. First and Current Jobs, by Class[a]

Percent

Job sector	1973–74		1978–79		1983		1988		1993	
	First	Current	First	Current	First	Current	First	Current	First	Current
Government	76	50	62	46	67	51	55	39	49	41
Private	11	28	21	38	21	30	21	32	23	26
Nonprofit	12	15	15	12	12	15	23	25	25	28

a. N = 200 for 1973–74; N = 231 for 1978–79; N = 171 for 1983; N = 192 for 1988; N = 196 for 1993.

underpin a pattern that will become much clearer later in this chapter: even when government recruits a top graduate, it is less likely to hold that graduate over time.

The trend is already well understood by students at America's top schools of public policy and administration, who know that many of the nation's most challenging jobs are now to be found outside the federal government, not inside. At Harvard University's John F. Kennedy School of Government, for example, less than half of the class of 1997 took jobs in government, with nearly a quarter going to the nonprofit sector. "Training for the nonprofit sector is one area in which public policy schools need to redirect their focus," writes Kennedy School dean Joseph S. Nye. "And those who enter the private sector will profit from an understanding of public policy, environmental issues, the global economy, the impact of the new technologies, and the development of public-private partnerships—many of which require a reformulation of the skills and knowledge we have offered students in the past."[1]

The trend is also clear among students just starting their graduate training. According to the 1998 George Washington Univerity study of nearly 500 first-year students in public administration, government remains the first choice of the students, but only barely. Asked to rank their preferred employers as they finished their first year in 1998, 52 percent of these master's of public administration and policy (MPA/P) students still put government first, with the federal government at 27 percent, local government at 15 percent, and state government at just 11 percent. The rest of the students were divided almost equally between the private sector at 26 percent and the nonprofit sector at 22 percent.[2] "Most MPA/P students do view Federal jobs as offering attractive benefits and job security," William C. Adams and his colleagues write of government's surprisingly poor showing, "but nothing else about such jobs is widely viewed as decidedly positive. . . . Even among those students who are interested, converting that interest into actual employment confronts at least one serious obstacle. Even students who are relatively eager to get a Federal job believe that doing so would probably be a prolonged and laborious process."[3]

As the following pages suggest, these trends reflect a broad shift in attitudes toward government as a source of what the nation's top public professions want most: challenging work, personal growth, impact, and advancement. To rewrite Cuba Gooding Jr.'s famous line from *Jerry Maguire*, the top students are saying "Show me the work," not "Show me the money." At least in recent years, jobs in government are looking less and less attractive, while jobs in private firms and nonprofit agencies are becoming more and more competitive.

The end of the traditional government-centered career involves more than just a change in first destinations, however. It also involves increasing motion across the sectors during a career. Significant though they are on their own, the trends presented in table 3-1 are the tip of the empirical iceberg. Once again, the classes of 1973 and 1974 help illustrate the pattern. Slightly more than half of the graduates who started out in government were still in government twenty-five years later, a fifth had left government for the private sector, a fifteenth had left government for the nonprofit sector, and another fifth had switched sectors a number of times. In the meantime, three-fifths of those who started in the private sector were still there twenty-five years later, but a sixth moved into government, and the rest became multiple switchers. The greatest movement came from those who started out in the nonprofit sector, where just one-sixth stayed put over the twenty-five years, while the rest split equally among moves to government, moves to the private sector, and a career of multiple switches. At least from what they said when asked if they intended to switch jobs and sectors in the future, the classes of 1973 and 1974 are likely to be the most stable of the graduates interviewed for this study.

Before examining this switching in more detail, it is important to ask where graduates take their first jobs and how they view the three sectors. As the federal government has pushed more jobs outward to private firms and nonprofit agencies and downward to state and local governments under mandates, it has changed its own image as an employer. To an increasing share of the nation's most promising public servants, the federal government provides what can only be described as a career of last resort, one that offers the opportunity for great impact on policy issues but at a high personal cost in frustration.

First Choices

The choice of a first job after graduation reflects a confluence of considerations, including family, location, job opportunities, and degree. Looking at all the classes combined in figure 3-1, public administra-

Figure 3-1. First Jobs, by Program[a]

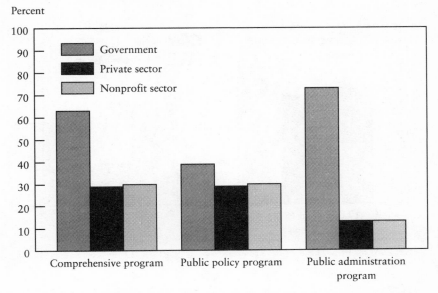

Percent

a. N = 653 for comprehensive programs; N = 125 for public policy programs; N = 222 for public administration programs. N = 231 for 1978–79; N = 171 for 1983; N = 192 for 1988; N = 196 for 1993.

tion graduates were significantly more likely than their peers to enter government for their first jobs, while policy analysis graduates were significantly more likely than their peers to turn nonprofit or private. The pattern is hardly surprising given the long-established links between the public administration schools and government at all levels, and the relatively younger links between the policy schools and social service organizations, public and private.

All of the schools have been affected by the erosion of the government-centered public service, however. Even public administration schools such as the University of Kansas, which has long been a premier supplier of city managers, began placing more of their graduates outside government. It is important to note, however, that the public administration graduates were slower to move. Looking at the pattern in figure 3-2, public administration graduates appear to have been much slower to move toward first jobs in the private and nonprofit sectors than were their comprehensive school and public policy peers, whereas public policy graduates were much faster. Unfortunately, the

Figure 3-2. First Jobs in Government, by Class and Program[a]

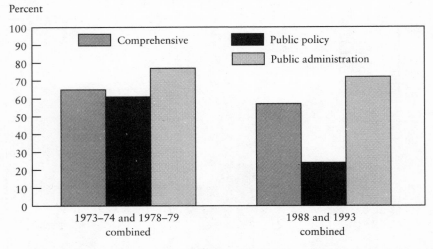

Percent

a. N = 431 for 1973–74 and 1978–79 combined; N = 388 for 1988 and 1993 combined.

subsample sizes by program and year are so small and therefore subject to such error that the shift from government toward the private and nonprofit sectors can only be measured by combining classes. Nevertheless, something seems to have happened between the 1970s and late 1980s to move policy analysis students toward the private sector. That something may have been the Reagan Revolution, with its focus on devolution and privatization, the rise of the consulting sector detailed below, the start of the federal downsizing, or even a dismissal of government as a destination within the schools themselves. But whatever the explanation, the shift accounted for a 37 percent decline in first jobs in government among policy analysis graduates by 1993.

As for the ability of the public administration schools to inculcate a commitment to government as a destination, the data presented here suggest that the socialization held for roughly two-thirds of their graduates. Seventy percent of public administration graduates who took their first jobs in government were still there when this survey took place, compared to roughly 60 percent of the comprehensive and public policy students who started out in government as well. Although small numbers of public administration graduates switch from first jobs in private and nonprofit settings into government, when all the numbers are combined, the warning to public administration schools is clear: roughly half of their students will ultimately spend time somewhere outside of government, regardless of how hard the schools work to create a preference otherwise.

Given their very real commitment to the government-centered career, the question is why public administration schools would be losing any students at all to the private and nonprofit sectors. Simply answered, the labor market for public servants has changed. Government is issuing fewer invitations to serve, while private and nonprofit organizations are issuing more. Much as they may prefer one sector over another, students must go where the jobs are. And the jobs are no longer as easy to find in government, particularly the kinds of jobs that graduates of the top schools want.

THE PUBLIC SERVICE MARKET. The classes of 1973 and 1974 could not have entered the job market during a better period for government employment. Exciting new agencies such as the Environmental Protection Agency and the Occupational Safety and Health Administration were still expanding, high impact agencies such as the National Aeronautics and Space Administration and State Department were still hiring, and the war on poverty was still going strong at departments such as Health, Education, and Welfare, Housing and Urban Development, and Agriculture, and states and localities were just heating up for a two-decade run as employment engines for new graduates. In short, government still had both the jobs and the missions to make a government-centered public service inviting.

The classes of 1988 and 1993 entered the job market at a very different moment. Virtually every federal domestic agency except for the Department of Justice, the Census Bureau, and the Federal Emergency Management Agency lost jobs under the 1994 Workforce Restructuring Act, which mandated a 272,900 cut in total federal employment. At first glance, state and local government must have looked like a much better market. Between 1990 and 1996, state and local government earned a place on the top ten list of growth industries. Local government ranked third on the list with 1.2 million new jobs, while state government ranked eighth with 200,000. As *Governing* magazine reported in 1998, state and local government accounted for more than one-seventh of all new jobs in the U.S. nonfarm economy.[4]

The growth was not even across the professions, however. Teachers and prison guards have never been more employable at the state and local level. The number of teachers increased from 3.5 million in 1975 to 4.6 million in 1990 to 6.3 million in 1996, while the number of corrections officers expanded so rapidly that it merited its own listing in the *Statistical Abstract of the United States* in 1995. Other professions did not expand so quickly. Jobs in public welfare increased from 354,000 in 1975 to 499,000 in 1990, but have stayed mostly flat since. So have the number of jobs for administrators, professionals, and paraprofessionals. Although state and local governments were still open for employment when the classes of 1988 and 1993 graduated, the hiring frenzy of the 1970s was long over.[5]

Some of the decline was offset by the growth of the nonprofit sector, which was just reaching a twenty-year hiring peak as the federal government began to downsize. From 1972 to 1982 the nonprofit sector grew from 4.6 million full- and part-time jobs to 6.5 million. Much of the growth came in health care, which added 1.1 million jobs, and social services, which more than doubled, from more than 450,000 jobs to nearly a million.[6] The sector grew even faster over the next decade, expanding to 10.2 million full- and part-time jobs by 1996.[7]

The expansion clearly affected graduate education. According to an ongoing census by Roseanne Mirabella, one of the principal investigators in the Nonprofit Management Education in the Year 2000 study, the number of graduate management programs with a nonprofit concentration (three or more courses) grew from just seventeen in 1990 to seventy-six by 1997. Roughly two-fifths of the concentrations were in schools of public administration, another sixth each in schools of business or social work, and the final quarter scattered throughout other schools.[8]

Unfortunately, the nonprofit sector entered its own crisis just about the time the class of 1993 finished school. Federal budget cuts and private competition were starting to bite into already thin operating margins, while a highly publicized United Way scandal had sparked a broad debate about the effectiveness and legitimacy of nonprofit organizations. According to public policy expert Lester M. Salamon, the budget cuts "not only increase the need for nonprofit services; they also reduce the ability of nonprofit organizations to meet these needs." At the same time, the private sector competition forced nonprofits toward fee-based services, which in turn "has put a squeeze on some of the 'mission-related' activities that have made nonprofits distinctive (e.g., charity care, research, training) and raised questions about the viability of the nonprofit form." In turn, the growing dependence on fee for service raised questions about the sector's ability to deliver services effectively, in part as a "reaction against what some see as the overprofessionalization of human services and the lack of adequate performance measures and accountability mechanisms in the nonprofit sector." Together, these individual affronts created a general crisis of legitimacy, driven not just by the United Way scandal, but also by what Salamon calls "a growing mismatch between the way the sector actually operates and the quaint nineteenth-century image that dominates public understanding."[9]

Given the tightening government job market and growing stress in the nonprofit sector, it should come as no surprise that the private sector might become a more attractive option for the nation's top public policy and administration graduates, especially given the increase in contracting out discussed in chapter 1. As government practices grew at private consulting firms such as Arthur Andersen, PricewaterhouseCoopers, and Booz-Allen and Hamilton, so did the effort to recruit top graduates. Deloitte and Touche even established a special recruiting program to target top graduates at Syracuse University's Maxwell School, Princeton University's Woodrow Wilson School, and the University of Pennsylvania's Fels Institute. With the freedom to offer $65,000 to $70,000 starting salaries and $5,000 to $10,000 signing bonuses, and the ability to make those offers early in a student's final year of graduate study, Deloitte and its private sector peers have an enormous recruiting advantage over government and the nonprofit sector, both of which tend to make their offers later and much lower.

It is important to recognize, of course, that private consulting firms occupy a tiny fraction of the labor market, accounting for a few hundred thousand jobs against a total presence of 18 million jobs for federal, state, and local governments combined. Metaphorically, however, the ability of private firms to skim the cream from the nation's top schools represents a new dimension to the end of the government-centered public service. With private firms such as Lockheed Martin and Maximus competing head-to-head for social service contracts that once automatically went to nonprofits, and the government practice at consulting firms such as Deloitte and Touche growing by 15 to 20 percent a year, it only stands to reason that the nation's public policy and administration graduates would notice.

THE SCHOOLS RESPOND. As the public service market changed, so did the top twenty schools. Rare is the school that does not offer at least some coursework in nonprofit organizations; rarer still is the school that talks about the government-centered public service as the only option for its graduates. Many of the top schools now offer courses in nonprofit management, and at least one, Harvard's Kennedy School, has recently established a separate concentration in the subfield. Although none of the schools currently offers any courses on running a government consulting practice, the course catalogs collected from the Internet suggest that almost all of the top schools have accepted a two-sectored service, government and nonprofit.

Consider how the National Association of Schools of Public Affairs and Administration markets the MPA and MPP degrees of its 240 member institutions in its beautifully designed advertising brochure:

> A Master of Public Administration or Master of Public Policy is the kind of graduate degree that can help you combine everything you learned in college—inside the classroom and out of it—into a truly meaningful career. One of these degrees is the credential for work in . . . legislative advocacy . . . nonprofit associations . . . charitable foundations . . . international affairs . . . service organizations . . . agency management . . . [and] every level of government imaginable. The career possibilities are the strength of the MPA and MPP. You'll find public affairs and public policy graduates making things happen wherever there is a public interest . . . around the globe or close to home . . . in huge cities and tiny towns . . . on the floor of the legislature and the streets of the world.[10]

Although NASPAA puts the emphasis on government, as do most of its members, it clearly includes the nonprofit sector as a viable career destination. And although NASPAA does not mention the private sector in its list of destinations, it appears to accept the option later in the brochure by advertising internship opportunities in "government, nonprofits, and the private sector" as an "integral part" of most programs.

There is a world of difference between acceptance and embrace, of course. Not surprisingly, given the data presented above, the public administration schools have been the slowest to embrace even a two-sectored service.[11] Nevertheless, among the public administration programs listed in the *U.S. News and World Report* top twenty, only the

University of Georgia talks of government as an exclusive career destination for its students. Far more typical is the kind of copy found in the University of Kansas catalog. After arguing that public administration, like medicine, is "a calling, not just a job," the Stene Graduate Program in Public Administration clearly demarcates its primary market as local government: "Since the program's founding, its primary mission has been preparing students for careers in local government, especially city and county management." And yet even the University of Kansas accepts the possibility that students might stray somewhat in the very next sentence: "Students can elect course work that prepares them for careers in state and federal government agencies and nonprofit organizations." One will search in vain to find the word "nonprofit" anywhere else in its web catalog, but at least the possibility is there.

American University is the more typical of the public administration catalogs, inviting prospective students to consider careers in organizations of any kind: "A public affairs education prepares students for a variety of careers. Graduates serve public or private agencies where they assist in creating or implementing policy alternatives ... Alumni are serving as city managers, lawyers, management analysts, investigators, legislative assistants, lobbyists, budget or systems analysts, newspaper editors, research associates, professors, and government officials, appointed and elected." Given the data presented below, the schools can hardly be fussy about where their students will go, particularly since the destinations have changed so dramatically from just two decades ago.

Perhaps because of its standing as both the oldest public administration program in the country and the top-rated school overall, Syracuse University's Maxwell School of Citizenship and Public Affairs has the toughest balance to strike in its advertising. It cannot undermine government, but it must also acknowledge the market. It does so on the very first page of its separate public administration catalog, where it tells prospective students that the "MPA is designed principally, but not exclusively, for those who plan to pursue careers in the public and not-for-profit sectors. The Maxwell School's MPA program prepares individuals for careers as managers and policy analysts in government agencies and organizations closely associated with the public sector." Maxwell also promises to help students find professional positions in a variety of settings: "federal, regional, state, and local governments; municipal financial institutions; public interest and non-profit organizations; and consulting firms."

Notwithstanding this ecumenical view of the job market, Maxwell uses its "signature" introductory course, "Public Administration and Democracy," to make a much more powerful statement about the proper and honorable role that government plays in a democratic society. Here, all first-year students are introduced to "the tensions inherent in *public* administration such as: the differences between public and private management; the competing values inherent in managerial, political and legal approaches to administration; and the marriage of merit principles and democratic responsiveness as it affects the public service." Although students are introduced to privatization, it is mostly through readings by Graham Allison on how public and private management are different, Ronald Moe on the limits of privatization, and former Independent Sector president Brian O'Connell on the risks of transferring government responsibilities to volunteer organizations. Maxwell's students may end up in the private and nonprofit sectors, but only after they gain a deep appreciation of the Athenian oath of service that graces the lobby of its original building.

Compare Maxwell's embrace of the multisectored service to that of the University of Minnesota's Hubert H. Humphrey Institute. Named for a leader who spent his career building the government-centered service, the institute has clearly concluded that the future is outside government more than inside. "A generation ago public administration schools educated students for work in government," the institute announces on the first page of the web catalog. "Now, when much of governance takes place outside government, many of our graduates find public service careers in not for profit organizations and private firms." The institute clearly sees value in a variety of destinations for its students. "For Humphrey Institute graduates, the road that starts in the classroom leads all around the globe, to city halls and state legislatures, to corporate America and international nonprofits, to Washington, D.C., and world capitals in the Americas, Europe, Asia, and Africa."

Minnesota's promise of private options is echoed by all of the top twenty schools offering public policy degrees. The University of Wisconsin's La Follette Institute, named after a public leader who spent his career dreaming up a beneficent and government-centered public service, announces that the "diversity of the positions held by our graduates—in the public sector, nonprofit organizations, and even in private business—testifies to the benefits of this flexible program." The University of Chicago's Irving B. Harris School even lists the private sector first in its program overview: "Our mission is two-fold: to conduct policy-relevant research adhering to the highest standards of social science and to train talented men and women for leadership careers in public policy, in either the private or public sectors."

None of the other top twenty schools comes close, however, to Carnegie Mellon and Duke in embracing the multisectored service. For today's student, the two catalogs offer a nearly perfect fit with what this report defines as the new public service.

Start with Carnegie Mellon's H. John Heinz School of Public Policy and Management, which offers an extraordinarily deep inventory of sector-specific courses such as planning and management of nonprofit organizations, as well as the kind of courses that are non-sector specific, such as leadership in innovation and organizational change that were once promised by the Yale School of Organization and Management. Although the Heinz School does focus its catalog on helping students manage organizations that operate in the public interest, its main selling proposition is the value of its degree for an ever-changing world: "perhaps the most important thing you can demand of a graduate professional education is a long 'shelf life.' After expending time, energy and money on your education, you should expect to carry away the analytic skills and intellectual framework that will help you succeed over a lifetime in an ever-changing global economic, technology and policy environment. The Master of Science in Public Policy and Management (MSPPM) program gives you a foundation in management and policy analysis that will be as valuable 20 years from now as it is in your first job after graduation."

Duke University's Terry Sanford Institute of Public Policy goes even further in embracing the new public service. The institute's message to prospective students is simple: "We are not interested in turning you into a narrow, number-crunching technocrat." And its director of graduate studies, Helen F. Ladd, makes the case for coming to Duke entirely around the training needed for "a career as a policy analyst and a manager in government, consulting firms, and nonprofit agencies." It is as if Ladd had the results of this study in hand when she began writing the following advertisement for her program:

Our graduates follow diverse career paths. The MPP is preparation for a wide variety of professional positions and, over the years, most Institute alumni take advantage of the opportunity for mobility and new challenges. You may start out at a federal agency, then move to the state or local sector, or vice versa. You may elect to work in a private consulting firm, and during the course of your career, move back and forth between the private and public sectors. The public service job market seeks people who have a solid foundation of analytical, management, and professional skills and who have a broad educational base on which to keep building and learning, and that is what the Duke program strives to offer.

Unlike the public administration programs, which have the student interest to maintain a mostly progovernment focus, and the public policy schools, which have found a substantial niche in the private sector, comprehensive schools walk a much more delicate line in trying to serve a much broader student body with a theoretically larger range of course options. As noted above, the Humphrey Institute has accepted the private destinations of some of its students, in part because it has moved somewhat from its original casting as a comprehensive school toward a much deeper embrace of public policy analysis. In contrast, the University of Texas's Lyndon Johnson School of Public Affairs tells prospective students that the "core curriculum of the LBJ School is designed to provide students with a basic set of skills and understanding required for effective professional performance in government."

As the nation's largest top twenty school, Harvard University's Kennedy School offers more opportunity. Its master's of public policy program, which is tailored for its less experienced students, advertises that "graduates will work in a broad spectrum of jobs, ranging from elective politics and government to positions in nonprofit institutions, research, and teaching," while its master's of public administration program, which is tailored for mid-career executives with at least seven years of experience, targets students who "are likely to achieve leadership positions in national, state or local governments, or other public-interest organizations, including the media and nonprofit organizations."

With a faculty so large that it merits its own search engine complete with a wild-card option for misspellings, the Kennedy School backs up its promise with a dense inventory of courses, including nearly two dozen offerings as part of its new concentration in nonprofit management.[12] Although the school does not advertise the private sector as a career destination for its graduates, Nye does tell his website's visitors that some of the school's 16,000 graduates do "guide the activities of private and non-profit organizations, particularly where they interact with the public sector."

The tracks of the new public service and old blend together in the two Kennedy school degrees. Twenty-seven percent of the MPP students interviewed for this report took first jobs with private firms, another 27 percent with the nonprofit sector, 24 percent with the federal government, 17 percent with state government, and just 4 percent with local government. The MPA students went in different directions, however, confirming the school's ecumenical embrace: 30 percent took jobs with the federal government, 24 percent with state government, 21 percent with the nonprofit sector, 15 percent with local government, and just 13 percent with private firms.

Such is the challenge of being a top public policy and administration school today. Some schools such as the Humphrey Institute manage the pressure by bulking up existing courses to include the nonprofit sector; others such as Carnegie Mellon cover all sectors simultaneously; and still others with the requisite faculty resources such as the Kennedy School create separate tracks for separate destinations.

REDEFINING TERMS. Troubled though they may be by the drift away from government-centered service, the nation's top public policy and administration graduate schools are not punishing students for embracing the private and nonprofit sectors, according to thirty-four in-depth interviews conducted with members of the classes of 1988 and 1993.[13] These graduates may not remember a proprivate attitude at their schools, but do not recall an antiprivate stigma either (Because the Kennedy School produces such a large share of all public policy and administration graduates, readers are forewarned that it also produces a large number of the quotes from the in-depth interviews discussed below.)

There is no question, however, that the top schools send subtle and not-so-subtle signals in favor of public sector employment. The

Kennedy School is so worried about the declining interest in government that it now provides $10,000 in debt relief for students who accept a federal Presidential Management Internship, while the LBJ School frequently exploits its connections with the LBJ Presidential Library across the courtyard. As one University of Minnesota graduate who took a first job in government remarked about the Humphrey Institute, "You walk in every day and there's Hubert Humphrey's desk staring at you and there's the Hubert Humphrey museum. And the people you meet as professors or the teaching assistants or the lecturers are all people who have dedicated their lives to public service. It's just part of the territory."

Yet, the fact that these are *public* policy and *public* administration programs creates a certain bias. Unless there is simply no room in the business schools, some graduates asked, why would a student go to a public policy school as a gateway to the private sector? "There was always an assumption that most people would work for government," a University of Chicago graduate noted. "It was a public policy school, after all." A Harvard graduate who started in a community development bank agreed: "I think there was some bias toward going to work in either the public sector or the nonprofit world. But I didn't feel any stigma toward those of us that chose not to. In my particular case I feel like my job almost straddled the fence. Maybe what I did was a little more acceptable in the eyes of some people. But I didn't feel any stigma." Nor did a Harvard student who went to government. "School was really, really good about the fact that it takes all kinds of people in all kinds of jobs and all kinds of functions to make the world go around. I don't think there was any pressure to go into the public sector." So was Syracuse, according to a graduate who switched from a first private job into government. "The program is geared toward the public sector and the course work while you are in the program is very public sector oriented. . . . But I would not call it pressure. I think they just want people to find jobs, and the public sector and nonprofits are more likely to be recruiting at Syracuse than Xerox and IBM."

More importantly perhaps, there is little evidence that the students themselves view private jobs as a betrayal of public service. Given repeated opportunities to criticize the private sector as a destination for their peers, the vast majority of the graduates took a "live-and-let-live" approach. This is not to suggest that all of the graduates were equally supportive toward colleagues who entered the private sector. "Some people just have to work in the government or private sector because of financial reasons," one Harvard graduate who went to the nonprofit sector argued. "I can understand that. I fortunately have the luxury to be able to work in a nonprofit because I don't have kids. I also think that having one-third of a class go to the private sector violates the mission of a school that is trying to teach public service. Now the people who go into the private sector are probably more public service minded for having gone to public policy school. They have a conscience, and will give money and donate their time to things. But I still find it very difficult that they are helping corporations make money and not doing a public service. Some of my classmates used graduate school specifically for that gain. I don't think there was ever an intention for public service."

Nevertheless, even when they criticized the sector, most of these respondents saw value in the experience. "It is sort of selling out a bit," said one Harvard graduate who started out in business. "But I think that there are a lot of good things people can do in the private sector and I think the private sector is what makes the world go around. The values that people bring to it are important and maybe people who are interested in public administration would bring good values to business."

A Syracuse graduate who started in the private sector but later switched to government offered a slightly different defense: "Just because I was working for a private entity does not mean I was not doing something that most people would agree had a major impact on the public. We were funded by seven different government levels and on and on and on. I was very public oriented even though I was not getting a paycheck from Uncle Sam. I don't see myself as having sold out." To the contrary, he was one of a very large number of graduates who spent their time delivering services under government contracts. His analysis was confirmed by the full survey: 30 percent of the graduates working in the private sector and 27 percent of those working in nonprofits said they spent at least 80 percent of their time on projects funded by government, while another quarter in each sector said they spent between 20 and 80 percent of their time on such projects. Going private and nonprofit increasingly means becoming part of the shadow government.

Alongside this acknowledgment of the realities of the new methods of service delivery, the classes of 1988 and 1993 also saw the private sector as an important learning option. "There is valuable learning and training in the private sector," said one University of Minnesota graduate who has stayed in the private sector. "If you transfer those skills and that knowledge and those habits to the public sector, you are doing a bigger service to the public than if you just took an entry-level grunt job at the Congressional Budget Office crunching numbers on agricultural subsidies for Northeast Arkansas. You've got to think big. To think big, you have to have big skills and a big reputation and in many cases a big ego." A Harvard peer agreed. "I think it's a pretty narrow-minded person who says private service is a betrayal of public service. The work I did in the private sector had as much or more impact than any number of jobs I could have taken in government for the public good. So for somebody to say that the only way you can put your public administration degree to good use is to go to work in the government, I'd say get up and consider other options, because I don't think that's the only option."

Other graduates saw the private sector as an intersection of sorts in the new delivery partnerships that are rapidly proliferating with government outsourcing. One Chicago graduate explained her job as "sort of the crossroads of economics and the legal system and regulatory policy. While it is a private sector job, a lot of the work is related to the effects of regulation and different policies on businesses and how they resolve those differences." Still others saw the private sector as the only place to go for community economic development.

Despite this ample rationalization, there was still an undercurrent in the conversations about the corrosive effects of making money on the public service ethic. Graduates who went to government and nonprofits saw the private sector as a place to go to make money and retire debt, and rarely criticized their peers who did so. But they also talked about the loss of self that comes with the larger paychecks and private-sector life-style. At the same time, graduates who went to the private sector often apologized for their decision. "Public affairs education is not solely for public service," one Chicago graduate argued. "One's career is a long thing. Opportunities for public service present themselves and can present themselves later as well." Asked whether private jobs can be a form of public service, the graduates were almost unanimous in answering yes. But they also wondered how long anyone could serve the profit motive without losing his or her public service bearings.

There is at least some evidence in the full survey to justify these concerns. When asked whether their *first* job after graduate school was a form of public service, 82 percent of the 1,000 graduates answered yes. Ninety-five percent of the graduates who started in the federal government characterized their first job as public service, compared to 92 percent for those who started in local government, 90 percent in state government, 83 percent in nonprofit agencies, and 71 percent in private firms. But when asked whether their *current* job is a form of public service, the numbers actually increased for all but those in the private sector. Ninety-eight percent of the graduates who were in local government at the time of the survey characterized their current job as public service, compared to 97 percent of those in federal government, 95 percent in state government, 89 percent in nonprofits, but only 40 percent of those in the private sector.

Some of those in the private sector were in jobs with absolutely no public service component at all, such as real estate and corporate law, while others may have soured entirely on the possibility of public service in private sector settings. The only circumstantial evidence that might prove the case centers on the broad switching paths discussed later in this chapter. Hence, only 38 percent of the graduates who started out in government and switched to private said their current work was public service, compared to 44 percent who started out in nonprofit and switched to private. Significant numbers of their peers appear to have made a clean break with all things public. In contrast, 100 percent of those who switched from private to nonprofit and 100 percent who switched from private to government characterized their current work as public service.

Views of the Sectors

The new public service involves more than the rise of the private and nonprofit sectors as alternative destinations for public service careers. It also involves a clear differentiation in what the sectors do best. The rising tide of federal outsourcing and devolution may have blurred the boundaries between government and its private and nonprofit partners, but these graduates draw sharp lines among the three sectors nonetheless. Regardless of class and current job, graduates of the top public policy and administration schools tend to view government as the sector that does the best job at representing the public interest, the private sector as the best at spending money wisely, and the nonprofit sector as the best at helping people.

WHEN WORLDS COLLIDE. Despite their general agreement on the respective capacities of each sector, the respondents still disagreed on just how much to trust government, private contractors, and nonprofit agencies to deliver services on the public's behalf. In a nearly perfect confirmation of Miles's Law, where one sits largely determines where one stands, at least if one sits in government or the nonprofit sector.[14] Asked which sector they trusted most, the graduates who worked in government and nonprofits were divided, mostly as one would have expected. Sixty percent of the graduates who were currently in government said they had the most confidence in government to deliver services on the public's behalf, while roughly half of those in the nonprofit sector said they had the greatest confidence in nonprofits.

It was the graduates who were working for private firms who showed the most ambivalence about which sector to trust. Exactly a third felt the most confidence toward private firms, while the rest of the group split between nonprofit organizations (32 percent) and government (22 percent), with a small number who simply did not know which to trust. They may see value in the private delivery of services, particularly in the fiscal discipline imposed by the market, but they also have general doubts about the effects of the profit motive on the public interest. As such, the graduates echo George Frederickson's dim view of the application of business practices to government: "If the dominant ethos or collective attitude in a governmental organization is civically inclined, then the emphasis on service, the greater good, the public interest, and effective government will be obvious. Conversely, if the governmental organization is increasingly served by those with private inclinations, who tend toward practices that in business are regarded as either acceptable or appropriate, but that in government are considered unethical or corrupt, then corruption will result."[15] (Frederickson is a professor at the University of Kansas, which was unabashed in its focus on training students for a government-centered service.)

As with their general confidence in the sectors, the graduates also agreed on the respective strengths of government, private contractors, and nonprofit organizations in spending money wisely, representing the public interest, and helping people. Given their academic pedigrees, it is not surprising that the graduates interviewed for this report know that the three sectors are not created equal. Each has its strengths and weaknesses.

There is most certainly differentiation in the survey data. Overall, 38 percent of the graduates said they trusted private contractors to do the best job of spending money wisely, compared to 33 percent who said nonprofits, just 15 percent who said government, and 7 percent who said all or none equally. Overall again, 59 percent said they trusted government to do the best job of representing the public interest, compared to 26 percent who said nonprofits, and 5 percent each who said private contractors and all or none equally. Finally, 52 percent said they trusted nonprofits to do the best job of helping people, compared to 30 percent who said government, and 6 percent each who said private contractors and all or none equally. The graduates were clearly drawing sharp lines, indeed.

At least on the surface, where the graduates draw their lines depends in part on when they graduated. On a nearly straight trend line from past to present, earlier graduates in the sample were more likely than were more recent graduates to trust government to spend money wisely (21 percent of the classes of 1973 and 1974 versus just 7 percent of the class of 1993), represent the public interest (62 percent versus 49 percent), and help people (35 percent versus 23 percent). Below the surface, the differences over time are substantially muted when the answers are controlled for where the graduates worked at the time of the survey. Because the classes of the 1970s contained a disproportionately large number of graduates who were working in government at the time of the survey, and because government employees are more likely to look favorably on government, the class-by-class comparison looks like a steady weakening of confidence in government.

Not all of the variation is explained by Miles's Law, however. As table 3-2 clearly shows, government has also lost confidence across the classes even among graduates who were working in government, as well as among their supposed natural allies in the nonprofit sector.[16] Much of the erosion involved only a few percentage points, but all in the distrusting direction. Graduates in government who finished school in the 1970s had more confidence in government than did their 1988

Table 3-2. Confidence in the Sectors, by Current Job[a]

Percent

	Current job sector					
	Government		Private		Nonprofit	
Confidence indicator and sector	Classes of 1973–74 and 1978–79 combined	Classes of 1988 and 1993 combined	Classes of 1973–74 and 1978–79 combined	Classes of 1988 and 1993 combined	Classes of 1973–74 and 1978–79 combined	Classes of 1988 and 1993 combined
Spend money wisely						
Government	26	18	13	4	4	5
Private contractors	25	35	53	59	48	33
Nonprofits	30	32	24	30	42	42
Represent the public interest						
Government	73	68	52	49	46	36
Private contractors	6	1	7	12	4	3
Nonprofits	10	20	26	30	42	47
Help people						
Government	43	26	25	16	14	18
Private contractors	4	4	10	11	10	11
Nonprofits	42	46	54	71	70	54

a. $N = 378$ for the classes of 1973–74 and 1978–79 combined; $N = 349$ for the classes of 1988 and 1993 combined. Figures do not add to 100 percent due to "all or none" and "don't know" answers and refusals.

and 1993 peers regardless of the measure, with the most significant erosion between the two sets of classes coming in government's perceived ability to help people. The erosion in confidence is also unmistakable among graduates who were working in the private sector, where government lost ground across the board, and among graduates who were working in nonprofit agencies, where government lost confidence in representing the public interest, but actually gained slightly in helping people.

It is hardly surprising that government employees would lose confidence in government. As citizens, they were exposed to the same forces that have eroded confidence across the board. Accordingly, they were no more trusting toward the federal government in Washington or their state governments than any other respondents interviewed in this survey. Only 9 percent of the federal employees in the sample said they trusted the government in Washington just about always, and only 11 percent of the state employees said they trusted their state government just about always. The only place that Miles's Law held was among local employees, who were roughly twice as likely (22 percent) to trust their local governments as any other graduates, in part because they were employed by those governments.

What is surprising, however, is the degree to which the graduates who went to federal and state government are so disparaging of their own organizations. Ordinarily, one would expect to find government employees to be more trusting of their organizations than of government in the abstract. That expectation holds here, too, but only by the smallest of margins. Just 20 percent of federal employees and 21 percent of state employees trusted their organization just about all of the time, compared to 33 percent of local employees, 37 percent of private employees, and 45 percent of nonprofit employees. One of two explanations could account for this lack of confidence. The first is that the corrosive effects of two decades of war on waste, bureaucrat bashing, and nearly constant reinventing have taken the greatest toll among those who felt it most strongly. The second is that federal and state employees simply believe their organizations are not to be trusted, perhaps because the two decades of war on waste, bureaucrat bashing, and nearly constant reinventing have not made those organizations any more effective.[17]

At least according to these data, the first explanation is the more powerful. Just 19 percent of government employees in the combined classes of 1973–74 and 1978–79 trusted their own organizations to do the right thing just about always, compared to 29 percent in the classes of 1988 and 1993 combined. (The classes were combined to increase the subsample sizes within each cell of the table.) Although this survey cannot tell where each class began, the data suggest that the past decades may have worn down government employees the most, even as the reinventings may have made government more hospitable as a place to work for those who entered from the more recent classes.[18]

More troubling perhaps, graduates who work in the nonprofit sector have become less confident with each entering class in the ability of their own organizations to help people. As shown in the two bottom right cells in table 3-2, just as most of government's loss among private sector employees went to the nonprofit sector, most of the nonprofit sector's loss among nonprofit employees went to government and no sector in particular. The decline is particularly sharp among more recent graduates, where the number of nonprofit employees who trust their own organizations just about always has tumbled from 54 percent in the classes of the 1970s to 40 percent in the classes of 1988 and 1993 combined. Perhaps because they have just arrived in the sector, they may be more sensitive to the crisis in confidence that Lester Salamon writes about. Whether they have become less confident because their organizations are under such pressure to become more like private firms is impossible to know.

Lost in these data is one small finding worth noting. The biggest gain in confidence about which sector can spend money most wisely came in the category of "all or none": just 2 percent of the classes that graduated in the 1970s answered "all or none" when this survey was conducted, compared to 11 percent of the classes of 1988 and 1993 combined. Given the other patterns in the table, it is most likely that "all or none" actually meant "none" to these respondents.

These competing views of the sectors offer important insights to the schools of public policy and administration, not the least of which is that their students may not agree on the merits of combining government and nonprofit management into a single class. Although such courses are convenient for overstretched faculties, they may be equally unsatisfying for all of the students, some of whom obviously believe that government is the wise steward of the public interest, while others believe it is a wasteful and unhelpful force. There may be perfectly good pedagogical reasons for offering joint courses on financial management, for example, including the generally accepted accounting practices that cross sectors, but the schools should be aware of the mutual suspicions between the sectors and teach accordingly.

The suspicions are particularly apparent in the in-depth interviews with the thirty-four graduates from the classes of 1988 and 1993. Although they had good things to say about the paths they took, they also had sharply negative images of each sector, including the ones that they occupied in their current jobs. In general, government was viewed as a place for big impacts and equally big frustrations, the nonprofit sector as a place for helping people and surviving stress, and the private sector as a place that makes fast decisions with little loyalty to its own employees.

GOING GOVERNMENT. Start with government, where the in-depth interviews revealed the deepest mix of opinions, both positive and negative. The good news was a nearly unanimous admiration for government's ability to create big impacts. "If you are able to shift a decimal slightly in one direction, it affects thousands of people," reported one Humphrey Institute graduate who started in state government only to exit for the nonprofit sector within two years. "There was a sense that you were really dealing with large groups of people almost to an extent where you did not know any of them personally because you were so removed and it was such a large number of people. I would be okay returning to state government, where you are slightly removed but are able to actually make impacts at a much deeper level." A Harvard graduate agreed in explaining his decision to go to government and stay there. "You get a sense of common purpose working together. You look at something that nobody said was possible, like a new school, or a new library, three or four years ago. And there it's standing and there are kids learning. Breaking through to somebody. Having things getting better. Being able to live with yourself." Another Harvard graduate who started in government and then switched to the private sector agreed: "It was motivating to get up every day and go to work and think that what I was doing was for the benefit of the common good, the everyman, or woman, as the case might be. That was very motivating and made me feel good and that's what it was about. My friends who worked in the private sector didn't have that feeling or that experience or that reality. That was something lacking for them."

The bad news is that the most positive statements about working for government came from graduates who had started there and left. As the discussion of sector switching later in this chapter will suggest, the reasons for leaving government ran the gamut from the lack of public respect to political instability. That Harvard graduate disagreed, for example, that government is somehow more stable than the private sector: "If you're in a senior enough position, the political leadership changes every four years or every two years. Every time the leadership changes your whole world becomes insecure because you don't know whether you're going to be kept or not. It is inherently less secure because of the built-in electoral process and its effect on the bureaucracy."

If many of the most positive comments about government came from those who left, the negatives came from every sector and career path. But some of the harshest comments came, again, from those inside government. Some graduates who were working in government complained about problems that attended making decisions. "You can't do stuff quickly," one Harvard graduate who started and stayed in government noted. "You've got to get all these people agreeing and sometimes they're people who simply won't agree because it's not in their interest to do so and you need their agreement. You can't just make a decision and stick with it, do it. You've got to keep messing around, messing around, messing around. And for somebody who likes to get things done, it gets really, really frustrating."

Others complained about the public distrust. "People make a lot of demands," another Harvard graduate said. "They can be very unfriendly towards you, almost seeing you as the enemy sometimes."

Still others complained about the distance from results. "The results or outcomes are not very clear," said one University of Texas graduate who went into state government. "The customer is pretty removed from my work. That link to seeing what happens is pretty weak. I would probably prefer to be more in the advocate position of working for something that I want as opposed to being totally impartial."

Some even attacked the civil service itself. "A lot of people in the civil service are so protected it's unbelievable," one Harvard graduate who joined a legislative staff argued. "You can be a total screwup and you still have a job. If you don't quit, you don't do any damage."

But common to all was a general view of government as a vast collection of deadwood, where their own units were the exception to the rule. It was as if the respondents had memorized the stock speeches of today's presidential candidates. "I think we don't do well in our civilian federal work force establishing criteria for advancement," argued a Harvard mid-career graduate who left government for the private sector. "In the private sector you don't advance unless you meet certain criteria, but in our civilian work force you promote people until they're totally lost." "I never considered a government job," said one Carnegie Mellon graduate who started in the private sector and later switched to a nonprofit agency. "My perception was that [in government] someone gets a job and moves right up the ladder. They don't really care about doing something as much as just saying 'This is my job and I do this for X number of years and I will have this kind of pension for my retirement.'"

She did not think much better of the private sector that she left either. "I think one of the things that I prefer about the nonprofit sector is that you don't have to deal with the corporate culture, which can be cut-throat. When you are worrying about shareholder return, sometimes your decisions are made more on a short-term basis for the betterment of the shareholder and not necessarily for the betterment of the whole. I guess that is one of the reasons I prefer the nonprofit sector. It is more humanitarian, if you will." Her conclusion was echoed among graduates who started in government and left, particularly those who went to the nonprofit sector. "I felt very removed from the actual people I wanted to work with," one University of Minnesota graduate said. "I felt that I wanted to be much closer to the population I wanted to serve. Very little of what I did in government had to do with actual day-to-day contact with people."

It is impossible to know how much of this bureaucrat bashing is simply post hoc rationalization for either leaving government or resisting the underlying bias toward government discussed earlier. But most of the graduates thought carefully about their responses and clearly understood the reasons for the red tape. "I do think that we are very fortunate in this country to have the safeguards available to us as a society, both by way of the courts and the democratic process," said a University of Washington graduate who started in the private sector and moved into a nonprofit advocacy agency. "So, yes it moves very slowly. I think that is more fair than not having enough input from the public. Yes, it is frustrating for somebody that wants to get things done chop, chop. Then he or she should go work for Bill Gates probably. The public sector is a very different culture. It is cumbersome and it is a pain in the neck, but I think in the long run it is more relevant. You see a bigger picture of life."

As for the familiar antigovernment tone, more than one graduate recognized the corrosive impacts. "It's degrading," said one University of Southern California graduate who started and stayed in the nonprofit sector. "I hear the comment 'good enough for government work' and see that statement as horrendous. Why are people interested in working other places than government? Because we don't put the value into government." Yet even he saw government as a distant destination. Asked why he had stayed in the nonprofit sector, the answer was his love of the organization and his commitment to the mission: "I believe I am part of this mission and part of this place."

GOING NONPROFIT. That sense of mission and connection was clearly part of the nonprofit embrace. Unlike government, which was characterized as a place to go for big impacts, the nonprofit sector was uniformly described as the place to go for one-to-one results and the chance to grow. The classic statement came from a Harvard graduate who has been in the nonprofit sector since graduation. "Nonprofits are there because there is a mission . . . a mission to complete. My career has to be very much focused on achieving something positive and I don't feel that can be done in the private sector for profit. I also think there is more freedom in a nonprofit. You get to do a lot of different things. You get to build a lot of skills that you cannot do in a government job. I was looking for a job that would definitely produce something, where there would be results from my work, where I could make a difference."

As the full survey shows, she was hardly the only advocate of nonprofits as the place to go to help people. Nor was she the only graduate working in the sector to criticize the private sector for putting profits ahead of people. "My personal values about what's important are what brought me back to the nonprofit sector," said a University of Minnesota graduate who had started nonprofit, switched to a private firm, than switched back. "I don't want to spend my life making a lot of money for someone else and I'm not really motivated to make a lot of money for myself either. I just want to use my skills to change things that I think are problems." His decision to switch back to the nonprofit sector after several years with a private consulting firm reflected his simple conclusion that "I don't think it is a good idea to make money off the poor." A University of Southern California graduate even talked about the role of mission as he struggled with leaving his organization to save a personal relationship. "It's a very difficult decision for me. I love this organization and there are times when I can't see myself ever leaving here. It's the mission. I'm so invested in this place. So I definitely struggle. I sometimes feel like I have to make an enormous contribution here before I can leave. When I put it in those terms it sometimes comes across as a jail sentence."

These respondents obviously understood the personal costs of going nonprofit. As that University of Minnesota graduate remembered his first job with a nonprofit, "I always had the impression that nonprofits are less dysfunctional than other organizations and that everybody is nice and that they care about what they are doing and believe in what they are doing, and that's not always true." As with the graduates who went to government, the harshest criticisms of the nonprofit sector came from within the sector.

To a person, the graduates who had stayed nonprofit complained about the stress in the sector. "I don't know of anybody I work with who sees themselves here for an extended period of time," said another University of Minnesota graduate. "Even executive directors don't see themselves in a place for more than five or six years. If they are the people with the most stability, you can kind of work your way down and see where the sector kind of collapses in on itself. It is a very high burnout thing." A Carnegie Mellon graduate agreed. "I think a lot of people start out idealistically and they are there for the cause, but whether they will stay depends upon the type of job they are doing and their individual situations—need for more time with family, money. There is extremely high turnover in just about any organization that I have ever worked in."

Some pointed to the fund-raising pressure as the cause. "There is not enough funding to feel like you can work less," the University of Minnesota graduate quoted in the previous paragraph argued. "As a result, you have people working really hard, who are underpaid, who are already working in an industry where there is high burnout because of the kind of job you are doing, especially if it is direct service. I think the combination of that makes people start questioning what they are doing after a year or two or three." A Harvard graduate who had switched from government to the nonprofit sector agreed. "Your ability to spend a lot of time on the mission is limited by the need to be constantly out raising funds. I think nonprofits grow up to solve problems and then when the problems go away they try to redefine themselves. The competition among nonprofits with similarly valuable missions and goals and volunteer boards and committed but underpaid staff, having to compete against each other constantly for the same dollars drives me nuts."

(Fund-raising was also a recurring theme among the graduates who had started with a nonprofit agency and left. Asked why he would not consider a return to the nonprofit sector, a Carnegie Mellon graduate who had left for a private consulting post focused on the money chase: "That grates on my nerves after a while. Not that there's anything wrong with earning money or anything. I just don't have the interest in begging for money any more. I've done it before and it's not fun.")

Others who stayed in the sector complained of the low salaries, lack of job security, poor board leadership, and ever-tightening government budgets, but the bottom line was always unrelenting stress and the turnover that followed. "This is an overworked, underpaid industry that is surviving hand to mouth," said a University of Minnesota graduate who had started and stayed nonprofit. "It is also an industry that can't focus on the larger issues of productivity and results because it is just barely surviving." Yet most respondents who went nonprofit were willing to accept the sacrifice. "I could see myself in a government job that might have paid double what I'm making here," that University of Minnesota graduate argued. "But the job would have been so narrow that I would have felt very disconnected. I sort of look at that as a trade-off."

GOING PRIVATE. The graduates who went to the private sector talked about a different kind of fund-raising, of course, but from customers, not foundations. Some of these graduates found the resulting sense of accountability energizing. "You can get things done much more quickly in the private sector," reported one Harvard graduate who had started in government and switched to a private company. "There is definitely a bureaucracy here, but when you are looking at the bottom line and you are thinking about how to satisfy the customer, you are very sensitive to making whatever changes are necessary. And I think that is a very different mind-set than in most public sector entities. It's very difficult at times for them to identify the customer and to look inside to make changes. It's not that they can't or haven't. It's just that they don't have the basic motivation for change."

Despite criticism from their nonprofit peers, the graduates who went private were neither apologetic about the profit motive nor noticeably less enthusiastic about their jobs. Although they did not use the language of mission to the same extent as their nonprofit colleagues, many celebrated the speed and agility of their organizations. "What was I looking for in my first job?" asked a Harvard graduate who started in the private sector and stayed. "A job that I would find personally enriching from a learning standpoint. That's number one. Number two, that I would be able to get up in the morning and be happy about working here. Third was adequate compensation. I'd rank that third." Her focus on learning opportunities was repeated by most of her peers. "The company I worked for had a product to sell," said one University of Texas graduate who eventually switched to government. "And that was something that I was just not familiar with. So I learned a lot about just the different ways you have to manage things when you've got that as your driving force. But it was still the selling of a product." A Harvard colleague who started out in government and switched to a nonprofit made no such criticisms in imagining a hoped-for future switch to the private sector, however:

I think that the way to be the most effective public servant would be to have worked in all three sectors. I think people who work solely in one sector, whether it's government or the private sector or the nonprofit sector, have a very narrow appreciation and understanding for the realities of those other sectors and it makes them less effective at interacting. And in government you need to be able to interact effectively with the private and nonprofit sectors. I have this bizarre idea, like mandatory military service. I think there ought to be some way to mandate that we all rotate through every sector because I think the lack of understanding and tolerance for each other's values and motivations and work ethics and methods leads to all kinds of problems that we don't need.

When asked whether taking a private job was somehow a betrayal of public service, a University of Washington private-to-nonprofit switcher was equally adamant in defending the colleagues she had left behind: "You are taking it entirely too seriously. If you get an MBA and work in a hospital, are you somehow betraying your business school education? That is hogwash. To me, we learn something from school and we are fortunate to have many opportunities when we get out." As a Harvard mid-career graduate put it, "The private sector can empower a person to do more good than he or she could do in the public sector, and I do not think this is all self-promotion. I also think I am kind of unusual and that it's unfortunate that so many private enterprises are missing the opportunity for public service because they don't look at the world in that light, and likewise that there are a lot of individuals who are committed to public service who don't even consider the private sector because they think of it as selling out."

Like their government and nonprofit peers, these graduates were hardly naive about the problems in their sector. "Decisions are rarely made because something is the right thing to do, or will really be the better long-term choice," said a Carnegie Mellon graduate who started in business and then moved to the nonprofit sector. "You see someone that has done a good job, that has been dedicated, that has been working hard, but for the sake of the shareholders, to increase their wealth, who has been let go through cost cutting because they have been working for so many years that they have a higher salary and higher benefits."

Nor were they always so enthusiastic about their lean, mean organizations. One graduate who switched from a small private firm to a corporate philanthropic foundation also complained about the bureaucracy. "There are times when it seems to me that people are simply doing their job so they have a job. And there is no sort of bottom line, no customer. The clients we serve are sometimes our own bureaucrats, so if I need something from the accounting department I don't get it for three weeks. The various departments within the organization are each fulfilling their own mission and are almost in competition with each other."

It was a view shared by a University of Washington graduate who had switched from a private firm to government, and in so doing had learned his own lessons about bureaucratic isomorphism (or what Senator Daniel Patrick Moynihan once called the iron law of emulation). "The private firm I worked for was not even a publicly traded company," he said. "It was just as inefficient and just as bureaucratic and just as full of red tape as the public organizations I have dealt with. To me, anything that is large becomes slow moving and bureaucratic. I think that is more a function of size than it is a function of what product or service you are delivering."

Graduates who went private also clearly recognized the trade-offs involved. "Employees in the private sector cannot and should not expect loyalty beyond just ordinary civility from their employer," argued a University of Minnesota graduate who went to the sector and stayed. "It's just the nature of a market economy. That's just the way things are. Get over it. Individuals in the private sector have to look out for themselves. You're there to make money and you're going to lose your job if you don't. So you can't expect any loyalty." A Southern California colleague who was considering a move into government offered her own horror story about loyalty. "I worked for one company that went through a regional downsizing that chewed up about 800 people in just two days. You had people working there that had started in the mail room and worked their way up the ladder. The company kept just 3 people out of 800, and the turnover rate hit 150 percent over the next three years." Nevertheless, she worried about government as an option. "Once you're off probation you've got a job for life, basically. I think that breeds employees who get comfortable with standing in place. I'm not sure I could take that."

Pay is no small part of the trade-off. To a respondent, all of the graduates who started or stayed in the private sector acknowledged higher salaries as a significant incentive. As one University of Southern California graduate who has stayed in the private sector explained, "I didn't have much choice when I looked at the offers. It's just that it would have been such a large pay drop and I was married with two kids. I couldn't afford to do that. And then a promotion came up at work, so that was even a greater pay differential as well as a good opportunity." Several also said that the private sector would allow them to land better government jobs later in career. But whether it was post-hoc rationalization or reality, most of the respondents also saw the chance to make a difference through their work. "The initial draw from the private sector was and still is the work," said a University of Chicago graduate. "While it was a private sector job, the work related to the effects of regulation on businesses and how they might resolve those differences in ways that could satisfy multiple interests. Pay was probably not insignificant, but it was also the challenge, the ability to make and affect policies."

As already noted in looking at the full survey, many of the graduates who went private did not see their work as public service at all. And there was at least one graduate from the in-depth interviews who clearly fell into that set. Much as a Carnegie Mellon graduate tried to characterize his job with a national shipping firm as a form of public service, his words rang hollow nonetheless: "I was fairly fussy about finding a company that provides a sometimes life-saving service, that has really transformed the world, that even though guided by investors who want a return on investment, still provides a benefit to society by delivering its services on time."

Yet, there was also a hollowness from time to time in the words of the government employee stuck in a dense bureaucracy who tried to justify the value of checks and balances for welfare recipients, or the nonprofit executive who worried about the self-perpetuating instincts of his organization. In short, the key to public service is not so much *where* it occurs, but *whether* it occurs at all. No one sector appears to have a monopoly.

A Service of Switchers

Sector switching may well be the defining characteristic of the new public service. If their intentions hold true, recent graduates of the nation's top public policy and administration schools will change jobs and sectors at a record rate. Convinced that it is unwise to spend too much time with any one employer, the classes of 1988 and 1993 were already ahead of their well-traveled older peers at the five year mark. Although there are life-cycle effects embedded in such intentions, the data discussed below suggest that today's graduates have already accepted the multisector public service as their career reality.

EVIDENCE OF INTENT. Consider four broad pieces of evidence on the intention to switch. The first indicator involves the simplest evidence of all. Asked whether they thought they would stay in their current sector for the rest of their career or switch sectors at some point, roughly two-fifths of the graduates said they intended to switch. The greatest intention to switch came from graduates who were in the private sector at the time of the interviews (47 percent), while the lowest came from those in local government (26 percent).

The intentions were not even across the classes, however. In all likelihood because they were at an earlier point in their careers and therefore less settled, recent classes reported a much higher intention to switch than did the classes from the 1970s and early 1980s. Whereas 63 percent of the classes of 1973 and 1974 said they intended to stay within the same sector during the rest of their careers, a third of the class of 1993 was ready to commit again. Even among those who say they intend to stay in the same sector, there are significant differences across the classes. Whereas three-quarters of classes of 1973 and 1974 said they intend to stay with the same employer during the rest of their careers, only a third of the class of 1993 was ready to announce such a single-employer commitment. Hence, one reason the intention to switch was lowest among local government employees is that the earlier classes had a much higher proportion of graduates who went into local government jobs.

The life-cycle effect becomes even more pronounced when the intent to switch jobs and sectors are combined into a single measure. Here, members of the class of 1993 were four times less likely than the classes of 1973–74 to say they intended to stay in the same sector with the same employer, and three times more likely to say they intend to switch both jobs and sectors sometime in their career. As figure 3-3 shows, they were already acting on those intentions only five years out of graduate school.

The second indicator involves views of the traditional one-employer career. Asked how many years a person should stay with any given employer before moving on, 27 percent of the sample said less than five years, 30 percent said five to ten years, and just 5 percent said more than ten years. The fact that the rest either did not know (36 percent) or refused to answer (2 percent) suggests a substantial pocket of uncertainty that would likely favor switching over staying.

Once again, intentions are not constant over time. In what appears to be another life-cycle effect, recent classes were much less interested in the traditional one-employer career than were classes from the 1970s and early 1980s. Whereas only 32 percent of the classes of 1973 and 1974 said a person should stay with an employer less than five years before moving on, 57 percent of the class of 1993 agreed. In what appears to be an effect of the changing labor market described early in this report, more recent classes are also significantly less likely to say that a person should work at least some amount of time in government during the course of a public service career. Whereas 42 percent of the classes of 1973 and 1974 say that more than ten years in

Figure 3-3. Intentions to Switch, by Class[a]

Percent

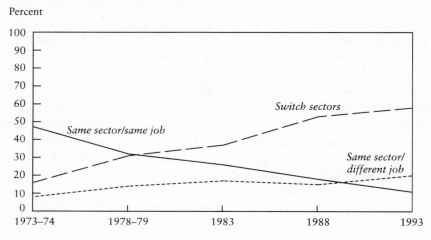

a. N = 200 for 1973–74; N = 231 for 1978–79; N = 171 for 1983; N = 192 for 1988; N = 196 for 1993.

government is the sine qua non of a public service career, only 21 percent of the class of 1993 set such a long mark. Readers should note again that large numbers of respondents answered "don't know" to this question, suggesting that a substantial but unknown number in each class (42 percent in 1973–74 and 40 percent in 1993) simply does not define government as essential to the public service at all.

The third indicator involves attachment to current jobs. When asked whether they were doing the kind of work today that they would like to be doing five years from now, just 62 percent of the total sample said yes, with virtually no difference across the three sectors or among federal, state, and local government. As with the other findings highlighted above, however, the numbers declined over the five classes. Whereas 69 percent of the classes of 1973 and 1974 felt settled in, only 55 percent of the class of 1993 agreed. The fact that the decline was not steeper suggests that the question may have tapped into more of an uncertainty about the future rather than a clear readiness to move.

It is also important to note that the graduates as a whole were highly satisfied working for their current employer. With exactly two-thirds of the graduates reporting that they were very satisfied with their current job, this relatively high satisfaction showed only a modest decline over time: 74 percent of the classes of 1973–74 were very satisfied compared to 62 percent of the classes of 1988 and 1993. This is not to suggest that satisfaction was even across all destinations and career paths. As this chapter will show, satisfaction does vary. Graduates who went to the nonprofit sector were consistently more satisfied than those who went to government or the private sector.

The fourth and final indicator of intention to switch involves images of alternative futures. Given the permission to imagine through the simple phrase "if you could choose," and asked whether they would rather work for government, a private business, or a nonprofit organization, only 63 percent of the graduates picked the sector they were already in. Roughly a fifth of the graduates who were currently working for government said they would rather work for a private business (10 percent) or nonprofit organization (12 percent), roughly a quarter who were currently working for a nonprofit organization said they would rather work for government (14 percent) or a private business (13 percent), and almost two-fifths of those currently working for a private company said they would rather work for government (18 percent) or a nonprofit agency (19 percent).

This general desire, perhaps even described as a longing, to be someplace else crossed the five classes, creating a pool of potential movers that spanned the decades covered by the sample. Within the classes of 1973–74 and 1978–79, which were combined to increase sample size, 63 percent of the government employees, 56 percent of the private employees, and 62 percent of the nonprofit employees said they would rather stay in their current sector than move. By comparison, within the classes of 1988 and 1993, again combined, 62 percent of the government employees, 47 percent of the private employees, and 60 percent of the nonprofit employees said they would rather stay put. Once the longing confronts the realities of job security, mortgage payments, and aging, the life cycle kicks in, of course, with the more recent classes much more willing to move than were their earlier peers.

The graduates who expressed a preference to stay in their current sector were hardly uniformly enthusiastic about their imagined future, however. All told, roughly a fifth of these "stay-put" graduates said they did not feel strongly about their preference, with the greatest reluctance coming from graduates in the nonprofit sector. While 16 percent of those who went to government and 17 percent of those who went to the private sector said they did not feel strongly about their preferred future, 30 percent of those who went to the nonprofit sector did not feel strongly about their imagined future, perhaps confirming the stress of being in a sector with the kind of high turnover and fund-raising pressure discussed below.

It is useful to note that the public service is not the only career marked by increasing motion. There is also spotty evidence that law and business graduates are moving more frequently. According to a tracking study of 10,300 law associates hired between 1988 and 1996, roughly 10 percent of the associates had left their private firm within one year, 27 percent within two, 43 percent within three, and 56 percent within four. Although some of the departures likely reflected the natural winnowing that occurs in such a highly competitive field, the anecdotal evidence suggests that associates at the nation's top law firms began cycling out as the allure of compensation wore off and the pressures of making partner took hold.[19]

Similarly, a 1998 survey of 2,200 master's of business administration graduates suggests that "MBA students seek to enhance their employability by working for companies that will serve as a good reference for their future careers and that will provide the tasks and opportunities the graduates need to expand their portfolio of skills." With the McKinsey and Company consulting firm as the top preference of the sample at 24 percent and the Boston Consulting Group as number three at 19 percent, many of these students are headed for careers with an inherent transience.[20] Business school professor Jeffrey Pfeffer views the pattern as a perfectly logical reaction to the changing employment contract:

> In the recent past, employees went to work for an organization expecting to stay with that employer if things worked out. The traditional, implicit "employment contract" was that if people worked hard and remained loyal to the organization, they would have careers and a long-term future in that organization, barring some economic catastrophe. Today, mobility across employers and even industries is expected. Downsizing, outsourcing, and the externalization of employment—the use of contingent work arrangements—reign supreme.[21]

The academic literature is just starting to address this reality.[22] Except for the occasional survey and popular article on the weakening of professional attachment, there is little systematic evidence just yet on what the new employment contract is doing to professional attachment. It seems perfectly logical that a decade of downsizing would shape career intentions. Whether those plans actually turn into reality is an entirely different question, however. It is one thing to imagine a career marked by sector switching, quite another to execute it. At least for the public servants interviewed for this report, however, the plans reflect an impressive, and some might argue troubling, reality. Graduates expect to move, and they mostly do. And, unlike the government-centered public service of old, the new public service offers ample opportunities to do so.

The following pages will ask three simple questions about public service switching: First, how much switching is actually occurring? Second, where does the switching start? And third, why do switchers switch?

SWITCHING RATES. The full graduate survey reveals what some may view as a relatively high degree of switching. All told, almost half of the 1,000 graduates interviewed for this report have switched sectors at least once. Of those who switched, roughly two-thirds switched just once, while a third has switched multiple times. When combined with detailed questioning on the places (meaning employers and sectors) and jobs (meaning specific positions with a specific employer in a specific sector) where the graduates have worked, the survey reveals at least ten different career paths within the public service profession:

—36 percent of the graduates started and stayed in government;

—18 percent have switched sectors more than once;

—11 percent switched once from government to the private sector;

—10 percent started and stayed in the private sector;

—8 percent started and stayed in the nonprofit sector;

—5 percent switched once from government to the nonprofit sector;

—3 percent switched once from the private sector to government;

—2 percent switched once from the private sector to the nonprofit sector; and

—2 percent switched once from the nonprofit sector to government.

There is remarkable diversity beneath this broad pattern, however. Consider four major findings in the data. The first difference in switching involves an unmistakable life-cycle effect: respondents from earlier classes were much more likely to report switching than were respondents from more recent classes. The simple explanation is that they have had more time to switch. Only 39 percent of the classes of 1973 and 1974 have stayed in the same sector over career, compared to 54 percent of the classes of 1978 and 1979, 50 percent of the class of 1983, 68 percent of the class of 1989, and 87 percent of the class of 1993. No matter how much they said that a person should not stay too long with any employer, the class of 1993 simply could not have switched as fast as classes with twenty to twenty-five years of service.

It is always possible, of course, that this apparent age-related effect is something else. It could be a generational effect unique to the baby boomers. Having suffered through Vietnam and Watergate, perhaps the earlier classes were less loyal to their employers. It could also be a period effect relating to the economic stresses of back-to-back recessions in the late 1970s and 1980s, and the burst in downsizing in the late 1980s. Having read the stories about downsizing in the private sector, and hearing the war-on-waste rhetoric of their own leaders, perhaps the earlier classes switched sectors in search of security.

Neither alternative holds when life-cycle effects are controlled by focusing on what the graduates did in their first five years of service. As table 3-3 suggests, the classes of 1988 and 1993 actually moved at a slightly higher rate over their first five years on the job than the classes of the 1970s, suggesting switching rates are likely to increase in coming years. "Life is a long path," a 1993 Carnegie Mellon graduate explained. "I mean some of the greatest government leaders or government people worked in the private sector, and the private sector has hired some very good government people. People, as the saying goes, deal with the cards they are dealt. You've got to think about your family. You've got to worry about the opportunities." Switching is simply part of the new public service package.

The second difference in career paths involves the three kinds of schools: public administration graduates were much more likely to have started in government and stayed put than were their peers, while policy analysis graduates were much more likely to have started in the private sector and stayed put. In all, 48 percent of the public administration graduates followed the government-only path, compared to 31 percent of the comprehensive school graduates, and 20 percent of public policy graduates, while 20 percent of the public policy graduates followed the private-only path, compared to just 11 percent of the comprehensive school graduates, and 8 percent of

Table 3-3. Switching Patterns in the First Five Years of Career, by Class[a]

Percent

Switching pattern	Classes of 1973–74 and 1978–79 combined	Classes of 1988 and 1993 combined
Number of employers		
One	53	46
Two	31	36
Three or more	11	14
Number of sectors		
Stayed in same sector	76	71
Switched once	20	24
Switched more than once	3	5

a. N = 431 for the classes of 1973–74 and 1978–79 combined; N = 388 for the classes of 1988 and 1993 combined.

public administration graduates. However, the warning signs to all three kinds of schools against specializing in any one sector are obvious: substantial pluralities of all graduates have become switchers. All told, 39 percent of the public administration graduates, 47 percent of the public policy graduates, and 49 percent of the comprehensive school graduates have switched sectors at least once, while 15 percent each of the public administration and public policy graduates, and 21 percent of the comprehensive school graduates, have switched twice or more. Given the class-by-class trend line discussed immediately above, those numbers are headed away from sectoral specialization and toward a much more mobile service.

The third difference involves demographic histories: women and graduates of color have somewhat different career paths than have men and whites. Whites were somewhat more likely, for example, to have gone to government and stayed than were nonwhites, while women were significantly more likely to have gone to the nonprofit sector and stayed than were men. To the extent that demographic diversity continues to increase, career diversity will continue to increase. Although men and women were almost equally likely to stay put by a margin of 56 percent to 51 percent, they were likely to stay put in different places: 12 percent of women started and stayed nonprofit, compared to just 5 percent of men; and 38 percent of men started and stayed in government, compared to 31 percent of women. And although whites and African Americans were almost equally likely to stay put by a margin of 54 percent to 59 percent, they were also likely to stay put in different places: 43 percent of African Americans started and stayed in government, compared to 35 percent of whites. Although the differences are relatively small, they echo the earlier warning about the problems facing any school that hopes to specialize in one career path.

The final difference involves public and private schools: graduates from private schools are not only more likely to switch than are graduates from public schools, they are also less likely to go to government and stay. Overall, 51 percent of the private school graduates (meaning the 435 graduates of Carnegie Mellon, Chicago, Harvard, and Syracuse) have switched sectors once or more, compared to 43 percent of the public school graduates (meaning the 565 graduates of Indiana, Kansas, Michigan, Minnesota, North Carolina, SUNY Albany, Southern California, Texas, and Washington). At the same time, only 26 percent of the private school graduates started and stayed in government, compared to 42 percent of the public school graduates.

There are several possible explanations for the patterns. One is that the vast majority of public school graduates in the sample come from comprehensive and public administration schools, both of which tend to favor government over other career destinations. The second is that private school graduates may carry greater debt into the job market, which may increase the attractiveness of private sector jobs. Recall that Deloitte and Touche offers starting salaries that are almost double the prevailing wage for entry-level posts in government, along with signing bonuses that can help pay down graduate school debt quickly. Whether higher entry-level wages and signing bonuses in government would change these career paths is not clear, however. As this chapter will argue, the decision to go private appears to be motivated more by the nature of the job at hand than salary.

WHERE SWITCHING STARTS. A central issue facing employers and educators alike is whether there is any pattern that might reveal a link between where a graduate starts his or her career and where that graduate finally lands. Does where one starts determine where one ends? The answer here is clear: graduates who took their first jobs outside of government, whether in the private or nonprofit sector, were more likely to stay put than were those who took their first jobs inside government. Of the graduates who took their first jobs in government,

57 percent were still in government by the time this survey was conducted, whereas another 17 percent had switched sectors multiple times, 16 percent had left government for the private sector, and 9 percent had left for the nonprofit sector. But of the graduates who started outside of government, 71 percent were still outside when they were interviewed, whereas another 14 percent had switched multiple times, and 13 percent had switched to government.

It is important to note the possible life-cycle effects embedded in this pattern. Because the classes of 1973 and 1974 had a very high number of graduates who went into government, and because those graduates would have been aging toward the years-in-service marks needed to secure full retirement benefits at the time of this survey, one could easily argue that government's retention problem reflects the perfectly natural pull of retirement incentives. Having received their public policy and administration degrees in their twenties and thirties, at least some of these graduates would have had ample time to cash out of government and start new careers on the outside, thereby creating the illusion that government cannot retain its talent.

The only problem with the hypothesis is that the switching rates out of government exceed the switching rates back in every class. As figure 3-4 suggests, graduates who started outside government were making a decision to restrict much of their future motion to the outside.

This pattern is particularly troubling if the basic concern is how to assure that government gets its fair share of talent in an increasingly tight job market. Simply stated, even when government gets a graduate from a top public policy and administration program, it seems less able to hold that talent than are the private and nonprofit sectors when combined into a single destination.

It is important to note, however, that private and nonprofit sectors are actually less effective in holding their talent than government when examined as separate destinations. Of all graduates who took their first jobs in the private sector, 55 percent stayed put throughout the period covered by this survey, 20 percent moved to the nonprofit sector, 13 percent moved to government, and 9 percent became multiple switchers. Of the graduates who took their first job in a nonprofit agency, only 46 percent stayed put, 21 percent switched to the private sector, 20 percent became multiple switchers, and 11 percent switched to government.

Figure 3-4. Career Paths, by Class[a]

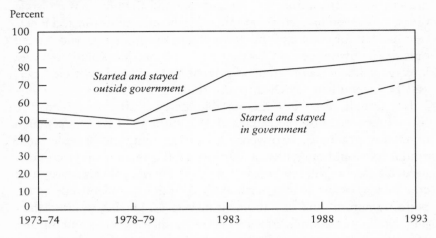

Percent

a. N = 200 for 1973–74; N = 231 for 1978–79; N = 171 for 1983; N = 192 for 1988; N = 196 for 1993.

This motion would have helped government but for the fact that most of the switching occurred between the private and nonprofit sectors, not between those two sectors and government. Once a graduate starts outside of government, he or she will very likely stay outside of government. It is a trend that suggests either a significant antigovernment ethic among these graduates or significant barriers between the sectors later in career. The available anecdotal evidence would favor the latter explanation. Bluntly stated, government appears much better at recruiting talented professionals at the front end of a career than at inviting higher-level talent into government later in a career. There are few job opportunities at the middle- and upper-career ranks in the federal government, for example, and most of those opportunities are used to promote internal candidates as a way to shorten the pay gaps discussed early in this report.

Although chapter 5 will offer more specific advice to government in combating these trends, it is useful to note here that there appear to be only two options for improving government's competitiveness in the talent wars. The first would be to make government entry-level jobs more attractive, whether through higher entry-level pay, signing bonuses, debt forgiveness, aggressive recruiting, or a long-needed polishing of the Presidential Management Internship program, which has tarnished with the passage of time. Although these options are well worth considering on their own merits, they are not likely to slow the trends described above. As the previous pages suggest, government's problem is not recruitment, but retention. And retention appears to be less a function of pay and benefits than it is of the search for challenging work and the opportunity to advance. Absent reforms that would make government careers more pliable and interesting, improving the recruitment process will likely yield an entirely predictable result: more top graduates will take their first jobs in government and leave at the first opportunity.

The second option is to make government jobs more inviting later in career, after the debts are paid off and after the first few years of soul searching are over. Since government will never be able to outbid the private sector, and since it is already subsidizing some of those private salaries through its own contracts, perhaps it should marshal its resources for a run at the top graduates later in their careers. Why not let the private consulting firms pay off graduate school debts? Why not let them provide the rotations that used to make a Presidential Management Internship so valuable? Unfortunately, below the 3,000 or so top jobs occupied by political appointees in Washington or the exempted positions in state and local agencies, government has never been particularly interested in filling its higher-level jobs with outsiders. Under pay freezes of one kind or another for the better part of a half-century, most of the middle- and upper-level slots go to the next employee in line.

Ultimately, neither option is possible without a significant reinvestment in government's human capital. If government does not have the resources to compete against the private sector at the start of careers, it will not have the resources to compete later in careers. If government at all levels is to become more competitive for talent, it must have the political support to compete.

Before asking why the switchers switched, it is important to highlight two more findings from these data. First, the nonprofit sector has clearly become a destination of intent over the past quarter-century. To the extent one can read between the lines in a large survey, those who went to the nonprofit sector in the 1970s seemed to do so more by accident than intent. Buffeted by the stresses discussed earlier, only

16 percent of the graduates from 1973 and 1974 who started in the nonprofit sector were still there twenty-five years later, compared to a retention rate of 54 percent for those who started in government and 59 percent in the private sector. The numbers inched up slightly to 20 percent in the classes of 1978–79, then jumped to 60 percent in the class of 1983, fell a bit to 54 percent in the class of 1988, and rebounded again to 67 percent in the class of 1993. Having started out with barely a third of the retention rates experienced by its government and private sector competitors, the nonprofit sector had clearly matured as a destination of equal holding power by 1993.

Second, as table 3-4 shows, career path clearly has a bearing on current job satisfaction. This analysis cannot answer whether a graduate's job satisfaction is another form of post hoc rationalization for having made a change, nor what a graduate's job satisfaction had been before the switch. Nevertheless, there is no question that certain kinds of switchers were happier in their current work than nonswitchers. Moreover, the data clearly suggest that staying in government is the least satisfying option for those who decide not to switch, confirming yet again government's difficulties in holding its employees over time. The data also hold a slender indicator of how strong the nonprofit sector can be in pulling graduates from the private sector. Graduates who switched from private to nonprofit ended up being dramatically more satisfied with their current jobs than those who switched in the other direction, while those who switched from government to private were actually more satisfied than those who switched in.

WHY SWITCHERS SWITCH. The public servants interviewed for this study switched sectors for a variety of reasons. Some simply admitted that they needed a change; others focused on family and finances; still others were looking for a better job.

The survey used two methods to find out why the switchers switched. The first was an open-ended question that allowed respondents to explain their decision in their own words. Although the number of respondents who answered was relatively low, 16 percent of those who did respond focused on career opportunities, 14 percent on a combination of frustration, boredom, and the need to make a change, 10 percent on salary and security, and 7 percent on the desire to make an impact. The rest of the responses to this open-ended question involved a mix of retirement, lay offs, family, relocation, further education, and the need to take care of a new business.

Table 3-4. Career Paths and Job Satisfaction

Units as indicated

Career path	Very satisfied with current job (percent)	Subsample size (N)
Stayed in government	63	300
Stayed in private sector	71	101
Stayed in nonprofit sector	77	65
Switched from government to private	72	90
Switched from government to nonprofit	77	48
Switched from private to government	61	23
Switched from private to nonprofit	81	16
Switched from nonprofit to government	63	16
Switched from nonprofit to private	53	32
Switched several times	67	168

This is not to suggest that switches across the sectors were driven by the same motives, however. Those who left government for the private and nonprofit sectors offered a somewhat different set of explanations for their move than did those who left the private and nonprofit sectors for government.[23] Only 14 percent of the graduates who left government for the outside world focused on career opportunities and a better job, compared to 25 percent of those who came into government on a switch; and only 5 percent of those who came into government from the outside focused on salary and security, compared to 12 percent of those who left government.

The second method for finding out why the switchers switched was to ask each one about a set of specific reasons that might have been important considerations in their decisions. Although limited by the fixed list of explanations, this approach generated a much higher number of responses. As table 3-5 shows, it also generated several significant differences between those who left government for the private and nonprofit sectors and those who came into government from either. Simply summarized, government's greatest draw was its ability to offer the chance to affect national or local issues, and public respect for the type of work the switcher would be doing, while the outside world's greatest draw was salary, with a slight edge to the opportunity for advancement. Otherwise, the switchers were in rough agreement on the underlying search for personal growth, challenging work, and interesting work, all of which appear to be in the eye of the beholder.

Table 3-5. Why Switchers Switched[a]

Percent

Very important consideration	Switched from government	Switched to government
Opportunity for personal growth	75	68
Opportunity to do challenging work	73	69
Type of work	64	66
Opportunity for advancement	42	36
Opportunity to impact national or local issues	39	58
Public respect	35	50
Salary	27	17
Benefits	23	24
Job security	16	19

a. N = 259 for those who left government; N = 101 for those who switched to government.

The subsample sizes get painfully small when the graduates who switched out of government are divided into those who went private versus nonprofit. So noted, the differences are exactly where one would have expected. Those who went private were twice as likely as those who went nonprofit (36 percent to 17 percent) to list salary as a very important consideration in the switch out of government, and somewhat more likely to endorse the opportunity for advancement (49 percent to 37 percent), while those who went nonprofit were significantly more likely to list public respect (54 percent to 32 percent), the opportunity to impact national or local issues (57 percent to 30 percent), and the type of work involved (83 percent to 62 percent) as very important considerations in their decisions to exit government. Neither group was particularly drawn to the job security offered by their new employers.

Similar findings hold for those who switched into government from the private and nonprofit sectors. Although neither group was particularly impressed by government salaries, those who came in from the cold of the private sector were significantly more likely than those who came in from nonprofits to list the opportunity for personal growth (81 percent to 56 percent), public respect (62 percent to 33 percent), opportunity for impact on national or local issues (72 percent to 44 percent), the type of work involved (73 percent to 56 percent), challenging work (81 percent to 56 percent) as very important considerations in making the switch. Reading between the lines, as a researcher is wont to do after soaking in the data, it is almost as if some of those coming to government from the private sector are seeking a kind of redemption from their past, giving up the higher salaries and opportunity for advancement of private employment for personal respect and the chance to make a difference in the world. No doubt many also felt capped in their current jobs. In contrast, those coming in from the nonprofit sector seem almost worn out by their work, ready to come into government to get a bit of respite from the stress described earlier in this chapter.

All of these explanations for switching are confirmed in the in-depth interviews with members of the classes of 1988 and 1993. Graduates who switched to the private sector from government talked about pay and opportunity for advancement, while those who switched back talked about the chance to make a big difference. "I almost think of my current job as field research," said a University of Minnesota graduate who started and stayed in the nonprofit sector. "There is going to come a time when I have identified certain barriers that need to come down. I could see myself going into government at that point."

But there is something more going on in these recent classes. Simply stated, these graduates believe that change is a natural, indeed inevitable, part of one's career. "Nothing is promised to us," said a Harvard graduate. "I have no clue where the next opportunity will come from, or which opportunity will present itself." A 1993 Carnegie Mellon graduate who had started in business and already moved once to a nonprofit offered an even briefer explanation of his stated intention to switch again: "Life is a long path and there are many forks along the way."

It was a view echoed by many of the graduates, including those who had not yet made their first switch. "One's career is a long thing," said a University of Chicago graduate. "Opportunities for public service present themselves across the sectors." Asked why she had not moved yet, she answered in what was a familiar refrain: "I guess I don't feel that I have exhausted the challenge and the opportunities for learning and the things that keep me entertained and interested here." A Harvard switcher agreed: "I don't think in this day and age, absent something like civil service, there is much employer loyalty. But it is also good to move around every once in a while. It gives you a fresh perspective on things. It keeps you from going stale." A second Harvard switcher pushed even further on : "I can only stay in a job so long until I just don't want to do that job anymore. I'll leave when I've learned everything there is to learn, when I'm getting bored with it, and when I decide enough is enough." "I'm a person who has always done a lot of changing," agreed a 1988 University of Washington graduate who had switched once from a nonprofit to a private firm. "That's stimulating to me and I like to be stimulated."

Switching involves more than the youthful hubris that professional schools of all kinds sometimes cultivate among their graduates. The intention to switch also reflects a clear-eyed view of the job market and lack of loyalty from employers in any sector. "I don't care if it is private or nonprofit," said a Carnegie Mellon graduate. "If you are not doing a good job or have a disagreement with someone on your board or one of your bosses or something, you are gone. I don't think the work force in general has much loyalty to their employers, but that is part of the environment that has been created over the last 20 years." A University of Southern California graduate who had started and stayed in the private sector was equally aware of the change. "The company I started out with was founded in 1777 and bragged that it hadn't laid anybody off in its entire 200 years. Now it is laying off employees all the time. Companies don't want twenty- or twenty-five-year employees. They are too expensive." Moreover, as a Carnegie Mellon graduate who had stayed put in the nonprofit sector argued, "all organizations are structuring their benefit programs around getting young, energetic people that they can work to death. Most people, especially those graduating from master's degree programs, are crazy to stay any place for more than five years."

Ultimately, the decision to switch may not be up to any of these graduates. Some states are contracting out welfare-to-work, while others are not; some federal agencies are contracting out regulatory impact analysis, while others are not; some of the most interesting public jobs are simply no longer available in government, while others have yet to be created with the advent of as-yet-unknown missions and technologies. Moreover, where a job is located at the beginning of a career may not be where that very same job is located only a year or two later. Some private firms will stay in the newly emerging welfare-to-work business, while others will most certainly exit or be bought out; some local governments will sour on private delivery and bring the jobs back in-house, while others will push even more jobs out. Who knows? It is a point well made by a University of Southern California graduate who started and stayed in the private sector:

> The job that I do now is available in the public sector. But typically in the past years, the private sector has been expanding bit by bit in my field, which gave me some security. That's changing now. My industry is going through consolidation right now, just like the banking and the financial industry more generally. Some positions are being eliminated or outsourced. And my company just got bought out. We'll see. If I get laid off, who knows? I'm not sure where I'll end up.

This uncertainty is part and parcel of the multisectored public service. Just ask Shannon Swangstue, a Humphrey Institute student and one of my former advisees. She began work in the Office of Personnel Management's Investigation Service in 1995 only to end up doing the same job for the newly privatized, employee-owned U.S. Investigation Services, Inc., under a sole-source contract in 1996. Obviously, she did not make the choice to switch. Who is to say she is no longer a public servant just because her employer switched sectors?

It is useful to consider one last finding in turning to the motivations to serve. Not surprisingly, the intention to switch is tightly related to satisfaction in one's current job. Just over half of the graduates who were very satisfied with their current job also said they were going to stay put in their current sector, compared to a third of those who were somewhat satisfied with their current job. Roughly 60 percent of the graduates who were very satisfied with their jobs in government said they intended to stay, compared to roughly half of the graduates who were very satisfied with their jobs in the private and nonprofit sectors.

It is not clear whether job satisfaction is the cause or consequence of the intention to leave, however. What is clear is that even the most satisfied graduates still report an extraordinarily high intention to switch. That is an extremely important signal to the three sectors on how the new public service works, too. Having concluded that no employer is particularly loyal these days, these graduates appear ready to move in search of the work they most want to do and the paychecks and benefits they most need.

The Motivation to Serve

If there is one constant among these graduates, it can be found in the basic motivations to serve. The graduates may come from different places and times, and may go to different destinations and career paths, but they mostly agree on what they want from work: growth and skill development, challenging work, opportunity for advancement, and interesting things to do. Some favor a bit more public respect, while others put more focus on salary and benefits. But those are mostly small differences. At the very top of the list of what they seek in work is the work itself.

A Focus on Mission

Graduates of the nation's top public policy and administration schools obviously want more than just any job. After all, most went to graduate school in public policy and administration for a reason. Although some students will pursue an MPA or MPP from a top school instead of an MBA from a lesser school, the vast majority of those who enter public policy and administration graduate school know they are headed into public work of some kind. "There are some who came to the Kennedy School who really wanted to be in the business school across the river, and didn't get in or whatever," a Harvard graduate described his class. "So they used the Kennedy School as a way to take a lot of business classes. And they were very antigovernment. And there were some that had been government employees who were coming back for a mid-career degree and they were going back. So they were like born and bred. And then you had the rest of us in the middle who sort of saw ourselves with the potential of moving in and out of the public sector, but always wanting to make a difference in some way." The key for most of the students interviewed for this report was not so much *where* they served, but *how* they served. "You've got to go where the opportunities are," said a State University of New York graduate. "If there aren't any jobs in your field, you have to do what you have to do."

This basic focus on mission emerged repeatedly in the in-depth interviews with the classes of 1988 and 1993. There is no doubt most of these graduates were motivated by a basic desire to change lives and make the world better. "I'm a child of the 1960s," said a Harvard mid-career graduate of his decision to go into government. "I was around when John Kennedy said, 'Ask not what your country can do for you.' That has always been important to me. I just felt being in the public service was better work, more honest work, helping people. It's just what I have always wanted to do." A University of Southern California graduate who went to the nonprofit sector agreed: "I've never had a job that was just a job. I want to be part of the mission. If you work in the Department of Motor Vehicles, you could look at that as just a job. But if you were able to make that experience better for the people who are coming in, you could make a difference in your own way."

Thus, most of the graduates interviewed in depth agreed that it made little sense to have gone to a public policy or administration school if they did not somehow want to have some impact on the public world. "Everything you're being trained for—how to manage without the profit incentive, how politics works, how to motivate employees without money, how to influence the public—is all directed toward the public sector," said one University of Minnesota graduate who nevertheless started and stayed in a private consulting firm. "I always just assumed that you go to a public policy program in order to pursue a career in government or the nonprofit sector. But there is always an overlay of public service and the spirit and the ethic of public service that the school didn't really have to try too hard to instill." That this student ended up in a private firm was a matter of luck and career planning. Having received a law degree in his joint program, he went into government, then moved to a private firm. But at the time of the interview, he was thinking seriously about moving back into government. "The reason for even thinking about going back in is the public service spirit I referred to earlier in the conversation. I was always really turned off by the notion of getting an MBA or going into a business and becoming a salesman or marketing type. There's nothing wrong with it of course. But personally, as a profession and life-style, it didn't appeal to me at all. I want to be somewhere where I can make a difference."

It is one thing to imagine such a job, quite another to find one, of course. Although there must be students who receive multiple job offers at the same time, the typical experience appears to be much more mundane and sequential. Jobs tend to present themselves one by one, and are accepted or rejected one by one. It is at this stage of the

Table 3-6. Motivations for First and Current Jobs[a]

Percent

Very important consideration	First job	Current job
Opportunity to do challenging work	80	77
Opportunity for personal growth	75	72
Opportunity to impact national or local issues	52	51
Type of work	50	71
Opportunity for advancement	47	46
Public respect	41	47
Benefits	25	41
Job security	21	35
Salary	17	38

a. N = 992 for first jobs; N = 716 for those whose current job is not the same as their first job.

process that the broad desire to serve gets translated into specific demands from the job. How well does it pay? What kind of work will I do? Can I move up? What kind of benefits do I get? Table 3-6 summarizes the list of considerations that the full sample considered to be very important in their choice of first and current jobs. Readers should note that the table examines only current job considerations for respondents whose current job at the time of the survey was not the same as their first job.

As the table shows, the nest of considerations becomes ever more complicated as one moves through career from first jobs to current jobs. Graduates are freer to ignore benefits, job security, and salary in the choice of first jobs, where challenging work and personal growth are the sine qua non of a good job. But as they age into second, third, and fourth jobs, the mix of considerations becomes more complex. Slowly but surely, benefits, security, and salary become more important in choosing the next position. So does the kind of work they are doing each day. A certain amount of boredom and grunt work might be an acceptable trade-off in a first job, but not later in career. Hence the dramatic increase in the weight given to type of work overall.

Of particular interest in the move from first to current jobs is the reluctance to give up the search for challenging work and personal growth. If this fixed list of considerations is a measure of overall motivation, these graduates want it all in a current job: benefits and security, challenge and respect, personal growth and interesting work.

They might have been willing to trade benefits and pay for challenge and growth right after graduating, but not when there are bills and mortgages to meet.

It is important to emphasize that the five classes were in close agreement on the motivations to serve in first and current jobs. It is one of the most important findings of the study. In the midst of all their other disagreements, the five classes were in tight agreement on the importance of challenging work, personal growth, type of work, and opportunity to impact national or local issues, creating a common bond in what has become an increasingly mobile profession. Notwithstanding the occasional variations by race and gender that were noted in chapter 2, the researcher is hard pressed to shake the agreement by any combination of demographics, work history, undergraduate degree, party identification, or ideology. Indeed, current salary is one of the few demographic measures that shows any relationship at all with job motivation, and then only in predicting the degree to which the graduates said salary was a very important consideration in taking their current job. Graduates who were making less at the time of the survey rated salary lower as a consideration in taking their current job than did those making more, an entirely predictable and not particularly important result.

As with the earlier discussion of switching, these findings hold important lessons for those who care about improving government's competitiveness in both recruiting and retaining talented employees. On first jobs, government's only comparative advantages over the private sector involved a slight edge on job security (24 percent of the graduates who took their first job in government said that job security was a very important consideration in that first choice, compared to 18 percent of those who took their first job in the private sector), and a significant edge on impacting national or local issues (55 percent to 38 percent). Beyond the edge in these two areas, only one of which government dare advertise lest it suffer the political backlash, the two sectors went head to head down the rest of the list, including virtual ties on the opportunity for personal growth *and* public respect (40 percent for those who took their first job in government to 42 percent for those who took their first job in the private sector).

For its part, the private sector has only two comparative advantages over government and the nonprofit sector on first jobs: salary (26 percent of those who took their first job in the private sector said salary was a very important consideration, compared to 16 percent for those who took their first job in government and 13 percent who took their first job in the nonprofit sector) and opportunity for advancement (55 percent for those who took their first job in the private sector to 49 percent for those who took their first job in government and just 33 percent for those who took their first job in the nonprofit sector). For its part, the nonprofit sector held its own with government on public respect (46 percent for those who took their first job in the nonprofit sector to 40 percent for those who took their first job in government) and the chance to impact national or local issues (56 percent to 55 percent) but trailed both government and the private sector on security, salary, and benefits.

At least for recruiting, it appears that government's greatest advantage is to put the focus on making a difference on the issues. It is a recommendation clearly seconded by other research on public policy and administration graduate students. According to a 1998 survey of roughly 500 graduate students at twenty-eight MPA and MPP programs across the country, federal government jobs are particularly attractive to students who want to have a "real impact on national issues." As the study argues, the attraction is "also stronger among those who value personal growth and job security and believe Federal jobs provide those virtues."[24]

On retention, government has a similar comparative advantage over the private sector. Government still had a significant edge over the private sector among those who were in government and saw the opportunity to impact national or local issues as a very important consideration in taking their current job. And it still held its edge on security. Where it gained ground slightly against the private sector was among those who sought public respect in their work: 52 percent who held jobs in government at the time of the survey said public respect was a very important consideration in their choice of that job, compared to 40 percent who were in the private sector. Otherwise, the three sectors stayed pretty much where they had been when these graduates took their first jobs after graduation. (Readers should recall that these percentages are for respondents whose current job was not their first job.)

The problem for government on both recruitment and retention in the multisectored public service is that the nonprofit sector has become an equal destination of choice on mission, and the private sector has become much more aggressive in advertising its significant salary and advancement opportunities. The findings presented above suggest that government might have its greatest edge in recruiting for talent later in career, when the private opportunities for advancement have leveled off a bit and concerns about job security might take precedence over salary, and when the nonprofit stress may have taken its toll. Unfortunately, to make such a mid-career recruiting strategy stick, government might have to sacrifice security. How else to create the openings for recruiting? The question is whether reducing government job security through flattening and faster career advancement would make government the employer of choice at both the entry and higher levels. Having built a system that provides life time security, government has little edge on providing the kind of work public policy and administration graduates want most. Perhaps a reduction in security would yield extraordinary dividends in opportunities for challenging work, which is a dead heat between the sectors. If, in fact, the secret to competing in the public service labor market is in the job itself, government could have the ultimate buyer's advantage.

Sources of Satisfaction

If job satisfaction is an appropriate measure of the fit between motivations and realities, then most of these graduates are in the right jobs. Two-thirds of the sample was very satisfied with their current job, and another quarter was somewhat satisfied. Only the tiniest fraction, 6 percent, declared itself only somewhat or very dissatisfied.

Despite this widespread satisfaction, there are variations within the survey. As noted earlier, some job paths yield higher current job satisfaction than others. Those who have either stayed in or moved to the nonprofit sector are the most satisfied of the graduates, no doubt because the sector offers such a tangible, if stressful, sense of mission and such immediate opportunities to learn and advance. As one Harvard graduate explained her decision to go to the sector and stay, "you stay with the nonprofit because you can see the results of your work. I am constantly learning. I am constantly gaining new skills. I am in an environment that is extremely positive. It appeals to the core of who I am. My work is doing something. The people that I work with are doing something positive and there is a consciousness of our mission."

Table 3-7. Job Satisfaction[a]

Percent

Characteristic	Very satisfied with job
Race	
White	68
Nonwhite	58
African American	62
Hispanic	55
Income	
Under $30,000	64
$30,000 to $49,999	67
$50,000 to $74,999	60
$75,000 to $99,000	72
$100,000 and above	74
Currently in public service	
Yes	70
No	62
Would like to be doing the same work five years from now	
Yes	83
No	35
Current job sector	
Government	65
Private	66
Nonprofit	75
Class	
1973–74	74
1978–79	67
1983	71
1988	62
1993	62
Sex	
Male	68
Female	66

a. N = 1,000.

Sector is not the only predictor of satisfaction, however. As table 3-7 shows, satisfaction also varies by race, salary, graduating class, and whether graduates see their current work as public service, but not by gender. The figure also shows that satisfaction is tightly related to whether graduates are doing the kind of work they would like to be doing in five years, which shows an entirely expected relationship between satisfaction and intention to switch. Although there are not enough graduates of color in the overall sample to permit much detailed analysis of the significantly lower satisfaction among nonwhites in general and Hispanics in specific, the pattern remains even after controlling for salary, class, gender, job path, and current location. No matter where one finds graduates of color, and no matter how well or poorly paid, they appear to be less satisfied than are whites. It is a pattern well worth further analysis.

The relationship between salary and satisfaction is easier to explain. These graduates may not be saying "Show me the money" in the choice of first jobs, but money does seem to talk in satisfaction. It might talk louder but for the fact that graduates earning $50,000 to $75,000 are less satisfied than their peers. One can only speculate on the reason. It could be that this salary range captures graduates who are stuck in middle-level federal government jobs, private employees about to be pushed out, or baby boomers dealing with middle age. This survey cannot solve the puzzle.

Ultimately, because the two variables are so highly related, it is nearly impossible to untangle the relative impacts of salary and job location on satisfaction. The most satisfied of all the graduates were making over $75,000 a year in the nonprofit sector (90 percent very satisfied), while the least satisfied were government employees making between $50,000 and $75,000 a year (55 percent very satisfied).

Conclusion

There is much to admire in the profile of the multisectored public service presented here. The new public service is motivated by the right goals, remarkably tolerant toward the alternative career paths that have emerged as government has slimmed down and pushed more of its work outward and downward into the private and nonprofit sectors, and highly resilient as the job market has shifted underneath it. Most importantly, graduates of the top schools appear to have accommodated the changing shape of government without losing touch with the public service ethic that brought them into the profession in the first place. Would that all professions could claim graduates that maintain such balance, even grace, in an increasingly stressful world.

At the same time, the profile shows a public service that may be entering a period of such uncertainty and motion that it may become increasingly difficult to hold on. Although there is plenty of stability in today's public service, particularly among graduates who went to a given sector and stayed put, there is also evidence of increasing motion wherever the graduates start. No matter how much one can admire the profession's agility, the increasing rate of switching implied in the intentions described above does not seem altogether healthy for building the kind of expertise needed for an effective public service. It could well be that the new public service will soon become another variant of the fast food industry, in which employees never stay long enough to qualify for benefits, let alone to build the long-term skills needed for effective leadership.

The profile also shows troubling evidence of rising stress, particularly in the nonprofit sector. Despite the sense of mission that calls so many nonprofit employees, it is not clear how long the sector can sustain itself with the kind of turnover described above, especially given the enormous pressure to compete with private firms for what were once nearly automatic contracts and grants. Philanthropic foundations, government agencies, private firms, and even public policy and administration schools all have reason to worry about the state of the nonprofit sector. Once the skimming of the cream of the current privatization movement is over, there will still be extraordinary needs to be met. The question is whether the nonprofit sector will have the talent left to accept the obligation.

All in all, however, this profile suggests that the public service profession is alive and well as it crosses into the twenty-first century. Although the profession is now scattered through the three sectors, it remains a deeply committed force for public good. And that is very good news indeed.

4

EDUCATING THE
NEW PUBLIC SERVICE

Students go to graduate school for many reasons. Some want a lift into a first career; others want deeper training later in a career. Some like graduate school so much they do it twice, returning for a second degree at mid-career. Indeed, a quarter of the graduates interviewed for this report went on for another degree, with the Ph.D. and law degree the two most popular options. "I've been through two graduate programs in public administration and they are amazingly different," one Harvard University mid-career graduate who is now back in graduate school for a Ph.D. explained. "The first one, the Kennedy School, really prepared me well for the rough-and-tumble work that I was doing right after. The graduate program that I'm in now is really preparing me for the greater depth and heavier analysis that I'm into now. Now, ten years later, I need another booster rocket."

Whatever the reason they went, there is no question that the graduates interviewed for this report were mostly satisfied with what they learned. Nearly half said their graduate program had prepared them very well for the different jobs they have had, while only nine percent said not too well or not well at all. No matter when they went to graduate school, what kind of program they attended, or whether they went to a private college or public university, most of these graduates were happy with what they learned.

Their satisfaction was not always with the content of the classes, however. Many of the graduates interviewed in depth from the classes of 1988 and 1993 pointed to the way they learned as the key to their career success. "Working in teams and with groups was very important to what I do now," a Carnegie Mellon graduate argued. "You have people who pull their weight and people who don't. You have that in the workplace, too. Might as well learn how to deal with it in graduate school." And at least one pointed to the hidden lessons learned from the teaching cases that are used in so many schools: "You had thirty-five type A personalities and were graded on participation," said one Kennedy School student about teaching cases. "So you knew you had to get something intelligent out there and get your air time and make that count. And so I learned that skill in being able to say something arrogantly a few times here and there. So you're not one of those windbags that goes on and on and on."

As the following pages will show, the top public policy and administration schools can be proud of how well they did in training their students. Graduates mostly believe that the degree has served them well as they have advanced through career. At the same time, the data for this report suggest that the schools can always do better, particularly if they listen to the graduates who have already arrived in the multisectored public service.

Before turning to this appraisal, it is important to note that the survey did not examine what appears to be a growing trend toward joint degrees of one kind or another. The Maxwell School estimates that one-quarter of its 1999 students are pursuing joint degrees in law, business, international relations, public health, social work, or the social sciences, while most of the web catalogs reviewed for this book advertise their joint degrees prominently. It is not clear, therefore, whether the lack of academic opportunities described below is being remedied by the students themselves through joint degrees.

Appraising Degrees

Students almost always get an opportunity to appraise the value of a course on the last day of classes, but rare is the opportunity to appraise the value of their degree five years or more into a career. Most institutions simply do not ask how well they did, letting their annual giving campaigns stand as an informal appraisal.

At least for the top schools of public policy and administration, the more formal appraisal embedded in the full survey is positive. Not only do their students believe the degree has served them well, they also believe that a student starting out today with exactly the same training they had received would be very well prepared for a public service career.

Not surprisingly, those with degrees from the 1970s were less likely than more recent classes to endorse their training as completely relevant for today, suggesting the value of ongoing mid-career education. But the numbers were high even among these classes. Exactly 40 percent of the classes of 1973 and 1974 said a student with the same training would be very well prepared for a career in public service, compared to 52 percent of the class of 1988.

Interestingly, the trend line breaks back downward for members of the class of 1993, where only 40 percent endorsed their training as the way to become very well prepared for today's public service. There are two possible explanations for the drop in satisfaction. The first is simply that members do not yet have enough data points in career to make a judgment about the value of their degree, while the second is a disconnection between what they learned and where they went. Recall that members of the class of 1993 were the most likely to have started their postgraduate careers in the private and nonprofit sectors.

The available evidence suggests that the second explanation is the more powerful. Satisfaction in the class of 1993 was actually quite high for the graduates who went to government: 52 percent of members of the class of 1993 who were currently in government at the time of survey said their training had prepared them very well for career, compared to 58 percent of the class of 1988 and just 38 percent of the classes of 1973 and 1974. In contrast, satisfaction in the class of 1993 plummets for the graduates who went to the private and nonprofit sectors, where only 33 and 32 percent respectively thought their training had prepared them very well, compared to 42 and 48 percent respectively for the classes of 1973 and 1974.

The disconnection holds when respondents were asked how well prepared today's students would be for public service careers having received the exact same training. Recent classes are significantly more satisfied with the value of their training *if and only if* they went to government, but not if they went to the private and nonprofit sector. The result is a curious combination of life-cycle and period effects in the same responses. Graduates from the earlier classes are significantly less likely to say their training would be valuable for someone starting out in government, which is clearly an expected life-cycle effect.

It is no surprise that earlier graduates would be the most likely to believe that the world has changed enough over time to render their graduate training less valuable. But these life-cycle effects simply do not hold for the graduates who went to the private and nonprofit sectors. As figure 4-1 suggests, the schools may need to rethink the ways in which they prepare their students for the nongovernment destinations in the new multisectored public service.

Nevertheless, the fact that so many graduates think so well of their training should be taken as an endorsement of both what the top public policy and administration schools teach and how they teach it. Even as the following pages explore areas where the schools might be over- and underteaching, nothing should detract from the generally high grades these graduates gave the top programs. Pressed to talk about how well their schools did, recent graduates were particularly accepting of the difficulties inherent in building a public policy and administration graduate program, difficulties that are embedded in the enormous diversity of experience discussed in chapter 2. "Part of the problem in this program and perhaps in many of the public policy programs is that each incoming class has a widely divergent set of skills," said a University of Chicago graduate. "They were coming straight out of college and others coming in mid-career, all with varying levels of analytic and quantitative skills. Each individual is going to have a different perspective on whether we are spending too much time on any particular subject. People who don't have a lot of experience with economics are going to feel like they want more basic economics, whereas people with a lot of experience are going to feel like they want to move on to more advanced subjects."

The challenge in building a top program is to find a balance between providing enough variety to satisfy the diverse abilities of incoming students and enough common coursework to build the core competencies and commitment that the public service profession needs. After all, schools do not exist just to create happy students.

Figure 4-1. Preparation for Public Service, by Class and Current Job[a]

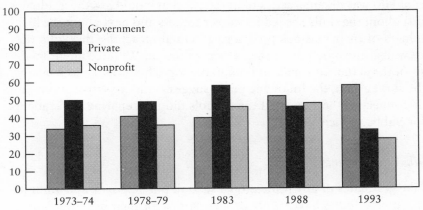

Percent very well prepared

a. Respondents were asked, "Now, imagine someone starting a career today with the *exact* training you received in your master's program. How prepared would this person be for a career in public service?" N = 200 for 1973–74; N = 231 for 1978–79; N = 171 for 1983; N = 192 for 1988; N = 196 for 1993.

They also exist to serve the profession itself, which may mean some level of unhappiness as students struggle with difficult classes.

The result is always going to be some level of dissatisfaction. "The biggest conflict was between one side saying that quantitative analysis was critical to effective government service and those who said that it was a complete waste of time," said one University of Minnesota graduate. "But the students who did well took it in stride and had a pretty good idea of what they wanted when they started. Those who had a very general, vague sense of what they wanted out of the degree didn't get much out of it. It required people to be self-starters. There were so many choices, it's so short, only two years basically, that you had to have a pretty good idea about what you wanted. Those that did cherry-picked the opportunities and the professors and the courses and developed a pretty good portfolio of classes and experiences that led to good jobs."

There are several ways to measure how well the top schools have done in providing the range of experiences that satisfy the multiple constituencies they serve. Ideally, one would ask employers how well the schools prepared the graduates for actual careers. After all, they are the end consumers of the curriculums. Unfortunately, lacking the resources to conduct such a far-flung survey, the best this researcher could do was design a series of questions that would ask the graduates first about the skills needed for career success and next about the helpfulness of their master's program in actually teaching the skills they viewed as most helpful in their careers thus far. With a content analysis of the actual curriculums used in the top schools as a check against the survey data, the following pages suggest a mix of satisfactions and disconnections in how well the schools did in preparing the students for public service.

What the Students Needed

Like graduates of any professional school, public policy and administration graduates have plenty of suggestions for their deans and directors about how to strengthen the curriculum. The only problem is that the suggestions go every which way. When asked whether there were any courses they wished their school had offered, most of the graduates interviewed in depth focused on "soft" skills such as leadership and management. "The courses that were most helpful to me were courses that helped me deal with differences, mobilize resources, and deal with people more effectively, particularly in a government or nonprofit setting," a Harvard graduate reported. "Those kinds of courses usually played second fiddle to policy analysis and statistics, which dominate the required curriculum." A University of Minnesota graduate agreed, noting that "a lot of things that we actually could have used in day-to-day life were shifted to electives. So people did not know what they needed until they got out and realized, 'Oh, if I only knew how public finance worked, I could qualify for this job or I would be able to better understand what I'm doing.'"

Yet, for each student who asked for more courses on leadership or more work in the core curriculum, there always seemed to be another who focused on the need for more quantitative methods or greater flexibility. Such is the nature of interviewing, indeed teaching, a diverse student body. "I think I was too general and too broad because I was interested in a number of things," said a University of Texas graduate. "So I fulfilled sort of the minimum requirements for quantitative methods. We didn't have a research methods course and

I think that would have been helpful. Even those people who weren't going into strict social science research could have used those skills."

Moreover, when respondents were asked whether there were any courses offered that they simply did not take, the answers ranged from more work on negotiation to advanced microanalysis. As another Harvard graduate remembered, "I could take courses anywhere in the entire Harvard system, including the Business School, Divinity School, Law School, you name it. It was all there. It was just a matter of waking hours. I probably had a choice of maybe 500 classes. It was scary." Asked how to choose among so many options, this student offered two paths: "Way one is you decide what would make you the perfect person and you sort of build your program around what your weaknesses and needs are. Way two is you find the most interesting classes on campus and you go to them. I took number two. And it was the right decision."

Even as one acknowledges the range in opinion among the kinds of individuals who enter public policy and administration schools today, the graduates interviewed for this report clearly agree on the skills that have been central to their career success. Asked to rate each item on a list of thirteen skills, the graduates considered leading others and maintaining ethical standards as the skills most important to job success. These results are reported in table 4-1.

Some readers will no doubt argue that maintaining ethical standards and leading others were bound to emerge at the top of the list because respondents have a natural self-interest in seeing themselves as both ethical and leaders. Simply stated, it would have been surprising had these two critical skills not been at the top.

Nevertheless, there is enough variation down the list to suggest that respondents did, in fact, do some sorting. It is hardly surprising, for example, that the graduates who were working in the private and nonprofit sectors would put so much emphasis on raising money and generating extra revenue. That is part of their very survival. Nor is it surprising that (1) graduates in local government would see managing conflict as somewhat more important to their success than did those in the federal government, since that is where the proverbial government rubber meets the citizen road; (2) graduates in the federal government might see managing a diverse work force as more important than did those in state government, given the remarkable success of

Table 4-1. Skills Considered Very Important for Success, by Current Job[a]

Percent

Skill	Government			Private sector	Nonprofit sector
	Federal	State	Local		
Maintaining ethical standards	81	75	84	81	89
Leading others	70	62	75	75	76
Managing conflict	52	54	67	64	66
Managing information and communication technology	57	54	67	64	66
Influencing policymakers	56	54	55	57	54
Managing innovation and change	52	53	55	57	57
Doing policy analysis	64	69	61	41	55
Budgeting and public finance	56	54	64	45	46
Managing a diverse work force	50	39	43	40	42
Analyzing and influencing public opinion	36	34	35	35	42
Raising money and generating extra revenue	17	21	19	34	51
Managing media relations	25	23	29	27	31
Writing regulations and legislation	37	35	23	22	22

a. N = 117 for federal, 167 for state, and 109 for local government; N = 275 for the private sector; N = 166 for the nonprofit sector.

the federal government in building a diverse work force to manage; or (3) graduates in nonprofit agencies would rate writing regulations and legislation so much lower than did those in the federal government, since writing regulations is so little of what nonprofit agencies do.

The fact is that most of the variation exists exactly where one would have predicted, given the differences in the sectors, which lends credence to other ratings on the list. Thus it might be reasonable to assume that these respondents, much as they want to see themselves as ethical leaders, may have put the emphasis on maintaining ethical standards and leading others because, well, that is what they see as most important to their success.

This debate over the veracity of respondent reports would probably not occur but for the two subjects that reached the top of the list. Ethics and leadership are considered among the most difficult, if not impossible, subjects to teach. Many schools have tried to develop leadership courses, but few have found great satisfaction in what they have wrought.

Nevertheless, at least three of the thirteen schools covered by this survey currently list some kind of leadership course in their core curriculums, including both Syracuse ("Executive Leadership and Policy Politics") and Harvard ("Political Advocacy and Leadership"), and four have full-blown core courses on ethics, including Harvard and the Universities of Kansas, Michigan, and Southern California. With its focus on the "ethical and moral dimensions of carrying out public policy," Harvard's core course on "Democratic Theory and Professional Ethics" is arguably the most fully developed of the four. As the course description promises, the course "explores the problems public officials face in balancing personal obligations and beliefs with the expectations of supervisors, colleagues, and the public, as well as with democratic institutions and traditions." Other programs may have leadership and ethics elsewhere in their curriculums, of course, but only a handful value the topics enough to make them part of the requirements for the degree, thereby increasing the likelihood that students will learn the right lessons.

Before turning to what the graduates think their schools taught well, it is important to note three other patterns revealed in the data by class that are not fully listed in table 4-1. First, there is at least modest evidence of a life-cycle effect in the skill ratings. Simply stated, the class of 1993 was the least likely on all but one of the thirteen skills, raising money and generating extra revenue, to list a given skill as very important to their career success. In four of these twelve skills, the difference involved only a few percentage points, as with maintaining ethical standards, where 81 percent of the class of 1993 rated the skill as very important compared to 87 percent of the classes of 1973–74. But in the other eight, the difference was much more significant, as with influencing policymakers, where 45 percent of the class of 1993 rated the skill as very important compared to 64 percent of the classes of 1973–74. But the general trend, leading almost always downward from the earlier classes to the most recent, clearly suggests that more recent classes either do not yet have the positions or the experience to know what was or will be important to their success.

This is not to suggest that recent cohorts have no clue about what they will need, of course. Recent classes may have disagreed with their elders in rating the thirteen skills as very important, but the final ranking of the top items was in the same order as the earlier classes. Moreover, at least some of the lower ratings have more to do with where recent classes went than with age. The fact that so many from the classes of 1988 and 1993 went to the nonprofit sector, and the fact that those in that sector have less responsibility for writing regulations and legislation, explain the significantly lower rating given by recent classes to the skill. Nevertheless, there is enough disagreement here to suggest that some members of more recent classes would not have been ready to learn the skills their elders have found so important, even had their schools offered the courses.

Second, whether respondents had stayed put or switched sectors had little impact on how they rated the thirteen skills except in three cases. Those who stayed put in any sector were somewhat more likely to rate managing a diverse work force as a very important skill (46 percent) than did those who switched (39 percent), while those who switched were more likely to rate leading others (76 percent), doing policy analysis (59 percent), and analyzing public opinion (41 percent) as a very important skill than were those who stayed put (69, 54, and 35 percent respectively). When combined with the lack of a significant relationship between these ratings and current employment, this analysis comes close to rejecting Miles's Law as a determinant of the perceived skills for success.

Despite these occasional differences relatively far down the list, the graduates shared a broad consensus on the top skills. The schools may face significant challenges in bringing such a diverse student body up to speed on microeconomics, quantitative methods, and government process, and they may need to offer more courses for students who are headed to the nonprofit sector, but at least they do not need to establish entirely separate degree paths for each destination.

Finally, graduates who had been reinvented the most were also the most likely to say that managing innovation and change was very important to career success. Only 46 percent of the respondents who had never been required to change how they worked as a result of a reform effort such as reinventing government or total quality management listed the skill as very important to success, compared to 56 percent of those who had been reinvented at least once, 62 percent who had been reinvented twice or thrice, and 66 percent who had been reinvented four times or more. Where one sits here definitely depends on how many times the chair, if not the occupant, has been moved over the years.

What the Schools Taught

The top schools of public policy and administration signal their views of what is important to professional success in subtle and not-so-subtle ways. Students certainly learn something from the course catalog, where deans and directors often wax philosophical about the changing nature of service. But they also learn from how the orientation session is structured, searches are conducted, faculty are promoted, and even how leave is awarded and sabbaticals are defined. It is one thing to write about the multisectored public service in a dean's letter, for example, and quite another to give faculty who take private and nonprofit sector appointments the same leave opportunities as are those who enter government.

There is no more important signal of what a school values, however, than the core curriculum itself. After all, the core curriculum reflects a school's ultimate authority to require a specific set of skills as a prerequisite for graduation. As figure 4-2 shows, the thirteen schools covered in this analysis have mostly exercised that authority to bring students up to speed on policy analysis and quantitative methods.[1] Of the 6.5 courses that constitute the average core curriculum, three courses deal with policy analysis and quantitative methods, a fourth centers on organization behavior broadly defined in this content analysis to include courses on organization theory, public and/or strategic management (Harvard's term) and general public administration, and a fifth involves public budgeting and public finance. The final one-and-a-half courses deal with a mix of courses ranging from leadership to policy process and ethics.

There is modest variation across the schools, of course. Carnegie Mellon, Harvard, and Syracuse all have relatively large cores, while Kansas, Michigan, and Southern California have relatively small cores; Syracuse packs its core into a one-year program, albeit one with two summers of study, while the rest of the programs cover two years; the policy analysis programs tend to spend more time on quantitative methods than do the public administration programs.

Nevertheless, students who attend just about any of these top schools should come away with a very similar package of basic skills. Almost all will leave with a rudimentary understanding of statistics, microeconomics for policy analysis, organizational theory, and public budgeting and finance. Beyond those basic skills, each student must

Figure 4-2. The Standard Core Curriculum at Schools of Public Policy and Administration[a]

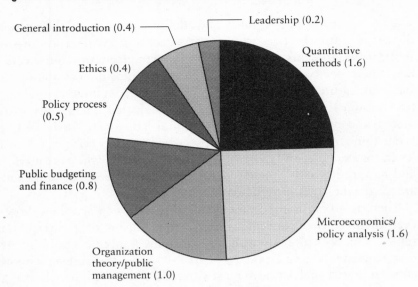

Source: Author's content analysis of core curriculum of the thirteen schools.
a. Segments show the average number of courses in the given subject.

chart his or her path. Students who go to Kansas will receive a more government-centered package, while students who go to Chicago will come away with a more private-sector-centered portfolio.

There is nothing wrong with spending so much time on the basics, of course. Law schools invest extraordinary first-year energy on torts, property, contracts, legal research and writing, civil procedure, constitutional law, and criminal law. However, because the standard MPA and MPP require just two years of coursework, a core curriculum of six or seven courses can occupy between a quarter and a third of total coursework. The proportion is even higher in the joint degree programs that most of the top schools offer. At the University of Minnesota, for example, joint law and public policy degree candidates spend roughly two-thirds of their one year at the Humphrey Institute in the core before exiting for a full three years of law school.

Moreover, turning back to table 4-1, the graduates themselves raised important questions about the relative weight given to policy analysis and quantitative methods in the core. If policy analysis and quantitative methods are two of the central markers of a professional degree in public policy and administration, why does doing policy analysis not rise higher in the list of skills needed for success? Should it not be closer to 100 percent? Even removing the soft skills of maintaining ethics and leading others at the top of the list, why are the harder skills of managing conflict, information technology, innovation and change, and influencing policymakers ahead of policy analysis? Should these subjects move to the core? If so, should others move out?

There are several answers to these questions. One is to expand the length of the standard public policy and administration degree to more than two years. That would create the room for a deeper core in what graduates say are the skills needed for success. The problem is that public policy and administration schools tend to compete for students mostly against two-year programs in business, social work, and education. Rightly or wrongly, they believe that an increase in time-to-completion would reduce the pool of applicants. A second solution would be to establish admission prerequisites in quantitative methods and microeconomics, thereby freeing one or two of the current core courses for other topics. The problem here comes from students with humanistic undergraduate majors—that is, the English majors, sociologists, historians, journalists, and so forth who might balk at taking community college courses in microeconomics and quantitative methods. Rightly or wrongly once again, the schools believe that admission prerequisites would either reduce the pool of applicants or narrow diversity.

Given this overview of the core curriculums, it should not be surprising that the graduates interviewed for this report might have concluded that their programs were not particularly helpful in teaching them many of the skills that they have found so important to their career success. While remembering their high satisfaction with the value of their degrees, the graduates clearly perceived important gaps between what they needed and what they were taught. Those gaps are summarized in table 4-2.

The table is hardly a perfect measure of what the schools do and do not teach well, nor of the disconnections between what students want and what they get. There is ample opportunity for selective memory in asking questions about what respondents learned ten, fifteen, and

Table 4-2. The Gap between Skills Needed for Success and Skills Taught[a]

Percent

Skill	Response: "school very helpful in teaching"	Difference between responses "school very helpful in teaching" and "very important to job success"[b]
Maintaining ethical standards	48	−34
Leading others	40	−32
Managing conflict	28	−34
Managing information and communication technology	27	−29
Influencing policymakers	41	−14
Managing innovation and change	33	−22
Doing policy analysis	65	10
Budgeting and public finance	48	−3
Managing a diverse work force	22	−21
Analyzing and influencing public opinion	32	−5
Raising money and generating extra revenue	15	−15
Managing media relations	17	−12
Writing regulations and legislation	26	−2

a. N = 1,000.
b. That is, question 25 less question 26 on the survey questionnaire; see appendix B.

twenty years ago, as well as ample opportunity to give their schools a dose of negative feedback for having forced them to take courses they did not like. "There's a reason we require these courses," an exasperated faculty member remarked after hearing about these gaps. "The students would never take them otherwise."

So noted, the table offers several insights worth considering as schools ask themselves how to educate students for the multisectored careers described elsewhere in the report. There is no doubt, for example, that the graduates believe their schools did a very good job of teaching them the skills needed to do policy analysis. It is the only skill where the students report more helpfulness than they needed. Even graduates who did not like the emphasis acknowledged that policy analysis is the current coin of the realm. "My academic program had a very strong microeconomic focus," said a University of Minnesota graduate interviewed in depth, "which is common these days in schools that want to be considered top of the line. But it cost me on the lack of coursework dealing with nonprofits. I don't think I took one class about nonprofits in my entire two years. The sector doesn't receive enough time for analysis. This fall I'm planning to go to law school because I think I can get the skills to do my job better. My guess is that students who go into the nonprofit sector feel that their programs helped them less than folks who go into government." Although Minnesota has added new faculty in the nonprofit area since 1993, when this respondent graduated, its new core curriculum remains heavily weighted toward policy analysis and quantitative methods, with seven of the eleven full- and half-course options focused on the two topics.

There is also no doubt that the gaps varied here and there for graduates who went to government, private firms, and nonprofit organizations. Although their current location had little influence on how they rated the helpfulness of their graduate programs, the fact that destination mattered to the importance of a given skill produced significant demand for coursework here and there down the skill list. Although it is risky to talk of relative frustration when so many graduates reported gaps on the list, those who found themselves in the nonprofit sector at the time of the survey reported the largest gaps down the list of skills. The gap was 41 percent on maintaining ethical standards, 40 percent on raising money, 43 percent on managing conflict, and 37 percent on leading others. That the gaps reached the widest levels for graduates who went to nonprofit agencies suggests that the schools may need to work harder at addressing the specific concerns of those headed toward the sector. It is not enough to simply retitle courses and concentrations to cover the public and nonprofit sectors.

Finally, in a repeat of the life-cycle finding discussed earlier, members of the more recent classes were usually the ones who saw the smallest gaps between what they needed and what they were taught. The gap on leading others and maintaining ethical standards, for example, was 37 percent each for the classes of 1973 and 1974, but just 23 percent and 20 percent respectively for the class of 1993. Unfortunately, these narrower gaps do not reflect a new-found emphasis on leading others and maintaining ethics at the top schools. Rather, as reported earlier, more recent graduates simply do not rate the skills as highly as their more seasoned predecessors, perhaps confirming again the ripeness for learning over time. Graduates simply may not know what they need until they are further along in their career.

So where have these graduates learned about maintaining ethical standards and leading others? Some of their learning must have come from classroom experiences in other subjects, where faculty and students model the hoped-for conduct. Some also must have involved the teaching cases, team projects, external consulting, and small group presentations that constitute the contemporary public policy and administration pedagogy. Finally, some must have emerged from the summer internships that most of the schools require for graduation. But as a general rule, these graduates would have closed the gaps identified above on their own, through on-the-job training, personal experience, and their own reading throughout career.

Given the ripeness for learning questions raised above, perhaps that is just as well. Students will learn when they are ready. Nevertheless, as the following pages will suggest, there is more than enough innovation across the top schools to supply the coursework needed to guide graduates as they learn in the future, even if they must do so on the job or on their own. The courses are available to any school that is ready to learn.

What the Students Could Have Learned

It is not clear just how far the schools should go to address the gaps identified above. Those that have put significant energy into putting more ethics into the core curriculum may wonder why their recent graduates have not noticed. Those that have struggled with finding rigorous ways to teach soft skills like leadership may decide to struggle yet again. There do seem to be at least two caveats about the data presented here that might form the basis for further discussions among faculties and deans charged with the always challenging job of curriculum reform, which has been compared to moving the bones in a graveyard.

The first caveat is that many of the gaps involve hard skills that can be taught. There is no question, for example, that managing conflict and information technology are skills that can be taught. The fact that students enter graduate school already adept at using computers and navigating the Internet is no excuse for the lack of deeper instruction on how to use information technologies as a management and analysis tool. And the fact that most faculties may not have much depth in conflict management does not obviate the need to build capacity.

The challenge for many schools is in finding the faculty ready to fill the gaps. According to a content analysis of the more general curriculums offered by the thirteen schools covered in this report, closing several of the skill gaps identified above would have to involve the development of entirely new courses. Although many of the schools do have courses on ethics, leadership, and conflict management ready to move forward from elective status to the core curriculum, few have much depth further down the list in table 4-1. Only five of the thirteen had courses directly or partially related to managing innovation and change in their 1998 catalogs, only four had courses on managing information and communications technology, and only three had courses on media relations.

As for those 500 options available elsewhere on campus, rare is the student with enough information to make wise choices from the course catalogs offered at most universities without at least some guidance from within his or her school. Unfortunately, if the in-depth interviews with the classes of 1988 and 1993 are any guide, many of the top schools do a barely adequate job of providing guidance to their own curriculums, let alone a road map to the many options available elsewhere on campus.

The second, more hopeful, caveat is that many of the schools are already making progress in filling the gaps with innovative courses. With most course catalogs open for inspection on the Internet, schools that want to borrow from each other as they seek to train the new public service can do so with ease.[2]

If they want courses that might help students headed to the private sector, they can visit the University of Chicago on the web and ask how its faculty teaches its basic course in finance, which promises to "deal in-depth with the central ideas and tools of finance," ideas and tools that "are largely independent of whether the context of the application is the public sector or the private sector." Or they can visit Syracuse and read the syllabus from "Consulting, Conflict and Change in Organizational Settings," which focuses "on the role and practice of the internal/external consultant as a facilitator for purposive organizational change."

If they want courses designed specifically for students headed to the nonprofit sector, they need look no further than Harvard University's Kennedy School, which has an entire concentration dedicated solely to the nonprofit sector. In 1998–99 alone, the concentration offered six full and five half courses, including a general introduction to the nonprofit sector, and courses on charitable foundations, social movements in nongovernmental organizations, the role of nonprofit organizations in forming public policy, management of nonprofit organizations, policies and practices in philanthropy, and organizational design in nonprofit institutions. If they do not find what they want at Harvard, they can always look to Carnegie Mellon, which has a small but highly focused list of courses that offer students a chance to specialize in the nonprofit sector.

When they are ready to move from destinations to the skill gaps identified above, they have plenty of options as well. If they are looking for courses to close the gap on leadership, they can look at the Kennedy School's course titled "Being a Political Leader," which advertises itself as "a how-to course in leadership for the political activist," or its offering on "Mobilizing for Political Action," which promises to strengthen a student's "capacity to act strategically and exercise leadership in rapidly changing political environments." If they want a bit more theory, they can turn to the University of Michigan for a syllabus from the "Political Environment of Policy Analysis," which promises lessons in "dealing effectively with the political environment of policy and administration," or ask the University of Texas for the outline from "Principles and Practices of Effective Leadership," which uses lectures, films, discussions, exercises, and case studies to examine the current state of research across the field of leadership studies.

If they want courses on ethics, they can browse widely across the growing inventory of courses now up at many of the top schools, whether the Kennedy School's "The Morality of Process," which promises that students will examine the "variety of legal processes societies employ—including contract, adjudication, mediation, legislation, voting, administration, and choosing by lot—and explores the values at stake in selecting one process rather than another to make social decisions and address collective problems"; the Johnson School's "Political Values and Ethics," which promises to "reinforce in both student and teacher the awareness that ethical considerations underlie virtually all political issues and choices"; or the Stene Graduate Program's core offering on "The Role, Context, and Ethics of Public Administration in American Society," which conveys George Frederickson's view of the relative strengths of government and the private sector in delivering services on behalf of the public.

If they are looking to close the gap on conflict management, they can visit the University of North Carolina website and read the outline for "Public Affairs Dispute Resolution and Consensus Building," which uses "exercises to develop skills in multiparty conflict analysis, negotiation, and intervention for intergovernmental, nonprofit, and community disputes." They can also examine the University of Indiana's syllabus from "Negotiation and Dispute Resolution," which promises that students "will learn the skill of interest-based negotiation through role play and simulation," as well as the skills of "mediation, arbitration, fact finding, early neutral evaluation, ombudsmanship, and facilitation," or view the outline for the University of Southern California's basic introduction to "Alternative Dispute Resolution."

If they are looking to strengthen their offerings in information and communication technology, they cannot do better than to visit the website of the University of Michigan at Ann Arbor and sample courses such as "Ethics and Values in Use of Information Technology," which focuses on the issues that "arise within the new information environment, the moral dilemmas faced by individuals and the policy implications for institutions as communities become familiar with, and adjust to, the impact of the new technological capabilities"; "Computers and Organizations," which promises to give students with at least some programming experience "a chance to explore the ways in which computers can fit into government," while introducing them to "the need for complete analysis of organizational structure, capabilities, and goals before attempting computerization"; or "Information Technology for Nonprofit Managers," which is a nearly perfect example of how to provide a sector-specific package of ideas. If they want a somewhat broader introduction, they might turn back to Syracuse and look at its "Computer Applications for Public Managers," a course that covers the "management of end use computing in organizations, data base design, implementation of data base systems, project management and public management information systems theory."

If they are looking to close the gap on innovation and change, they can find a remarkable inventory of courses at Carnegie Mellon, including "Organizational Change: Transition and Transformation," which offers insights on "managing disruptions from transitions and the inevitable losses that change brings"; and "Innovation and Organizational Change," which starts with "models of leadership and change in public and private institutions" and ends with "the unique

problems faced by leaders attempting major institutional change."
Although the University of California, Berkeley, was not part of this
study sample, one cannot resist suggesting a look at its course titled
"Organizational Decline and Cutback Management," which analyzes
the "differences in the response of public and private organizations to
fiscal stress, with attention to the threat posed by organizational
decline to traditional pluralistic politics."

If schools need a course on managing a diverse work force, they can
peruse Carnegie Mellon's outline for "Managing in a Multicultural
Society," which is designed to help students understand how "to com-
municate with and manage people who are culturally different," as
well as the University of Texas syllabus on "Managing Diversity,"
which "is designed to acquaint students with the variety of groups
and personal orientations they may encounter during the course of a
professional career and to provide insights into their differing histories
and life experiences."

Finally, if they are particularly concerned about closing the gap on
nonprofit fund-raising, they can review the outline for Carnegie Mellon's course on "Resource Development for Nonprofit Organizations," a primer on assuring "that the organization you manage has
the financial and human resources necessary to carry out its mission
and maintain organizational financial stability." Or they can go back
to the University of Chicago website and see how its faculty teaches
government and nonprofit accounting as a unified course in generally
accepted accounting principles. Or they can reach even further into
the upper Midwest and look at the University of Minnesota's course
on nonprofit governance, which is designed to help students understand "the governance systems, strategic management practices, impact of different funding environments, and management of multiple
constituencies" that make managing nonprofits so difficult compared
to other organizations. They might also take a look at the course on
"Government Grant and Proposal Writing" offered by the State
University of New York, Albany, which promises to teach students
headed toward any sector lessons on how to tap government funding.

The fact is that the top schools have done a remarkable job of
building innovative curriculums that meet every need their graduates
identified. The only thing a curriculum committee need do is to turn
on the computer and start surfing the Internet to find the appropriate

syllabus, then identify a faculty member ready to take on the task. It is that simple.

Conclusion

Everything a professional school does for its graduates does not necessarily occur in the two years when its students are in residence. Much as they applaud the value of their degrees, the graduates interviewed for this report clearly recognize that educational experience continues years into the future.

Unfortunately, these respondents had little to say about what their schools have done for them lately, in part because many of the schools have neither the resources nor enrollments to maintain the kinds of alumni chapters and networks so prevalent in the business and law schools. As suggested in appendix A, the alumni directories used for this report carried very high error rates, which suggests that the schools may be having some difficulty in following their own graduates. Moreover, the American Society of Public Administration, which is the only membership association directly aimed at the public service, remains mostly distant from the public policy schools and has never been a strong presence for those who enter the private or nonprofit sector.

Even as one acknowledges the difficulties in building networks for a multisector public service, many of the graduates interviewed here clearly long for the chance to share information. "It would be wonderful if there were an association of professional public service graduates that really worked at cultivating relationships and keeping those people in touch with each other," said a 1988 Harvard graduate who had an MBA from one side of the Charles and an MPA from the other. "Partly that's because people who go to these kinds of schools are by their nature more willing to help and to share and to cooperate than are people who go to business school. I'm not blaming anybody for that. But it would be useful if there were some kind of postgraduate organization to which we could all belong and share information and ideas and addresses and phone numbers." "To use a buzzword from business," said a University of Minnesota graduate, "networking is critical when you get to the middle levels of career. That's where whom you know starts becoming very critical, and where the contacts you have can help you move up. So how schools can best help people at this stage in their lives is to have pretty active and vigorous alumni programs, newsletters, e-mail lists, and encourage people to get together here and there."

Although many of the schools offer these kinds of networking experiences, the desire for more networking may signal a broader need for guidance as these graduates navigate the volatile careers that constitute the new public service. Much as they accept, even embrace, the job and sector switching inherent in the new public service, even graduates of the top schools need help in career planning, whether in choosing their first jobs or in making mid-career changes. As this study clearly suggests, there are consequences in making those choices. Where graduates begin their careers has some impact on where they end up, and how they move across the sectors has at least some bearing on their overall job satisfaction.

Without criticizing their programs, the graduates seem to be asking for a little more help in setting their compasses from time to time. Whether this would require more career counseling when they are in school or stronger alumni networking, occasional mid-career refreshers or even the creation of an entirely new organization after graduation is not clear.

What is clear from the in-depth interviews is that these graduates are generally satisfied with where they have been and where they intend to be going, but still long for occasional contact with fellow professionals who are part of the multisectored service. They could also be of considerable help as their schools seek to design programs that give future students the maximum advantage in what has become a much more uncertain profession.

5

EMBRACING THE
NEW PUBLIC SERVICE

Absent some unexpected, highly improbable reversal in the trends described earlier in this book, the government-centered public service is gone for good. The federal government is not going to stop pushing responsibilities down to the states and localities, states are not going to stop pushing responsibilities down to the localities, and localities are not going to stop pushing responsibilities out to nonprofits. Nor are federal, state, and local governments going to stop contracting out to private firms. Driven by unrelenting pressure to stay small, governments at all levels have created an ever-growing shadow of private and nonprofit employees that produce many of the goods and services once delivered in-house.

The rise of the multisectored public service involves more than a grand conceit to hide the true size of government, however. The nonprofit sector has been growing for the better part of three decades, while the federal government has long relied on private contractors as the backbone of its research and development effort. What makes the 1990s different is the pace with which governments are turning to private and nonprofit sources. Keeping government small has become the reform for all persuasions. It gives Democrats maneuvering room for activism, Republicans an opportunity to create private jobs, Congress a needed source of campaign contributions, and the president a way to regain at least some control over the administrative hierarchy. Even middle-level civil servants appear to benefit from keeping government small. At least over the last fifteen years of steady downsizing, their average grade has gone up and their performance appraisals have never been better.

A government that looks smaller and delivers more is not the only reason the multisector public service is here to stay, however. There is plenty of fuel for continued growth in the number of nonprofit jobs as charitable contributions set yearly records and new philanthropies emerge almost weekly. There is also room for growth in the private consulting industry, where government practice has been growing by 20 to 25 percent a year. Unable to offer competitive salaries across the board, all levels of government are doing what comes naturally: buying the needed capacity wherever they can find it.

The question for this final chapter is not whether the multisectored public service is here to stay, however, but how students, graduates, schools of public policy and administration, government, and the nonprofit sector deal with the new realities. The private sector already knows what it is going to do. It is going to show up on campus early, offer high salaries and signing bonuses, and follow up with significant opportunities for advancement and challenging work. Before asking how each of these participants should respond to the public service, it is useful to review the findings of the study presented in this book, if only because the changes outlined here have been so steady that they may have been missed.

Review

The trend lines described in this book are clear. Government is no longer the primary destination of choice for graduates of the top public policy schools. The nonprofit and private sectors are, providing more than half of the first jobs for graduates of the class of 1993. When the destinations are divided by levels of government, the federal government ran dead last as a first job for members of the class of 1993, while the nonprofit and private sectors ran first and second respectively. Government is not out of the running, of course, but it most certainly now faces very strong competition. If government cannot recruit a majority of students who have made public service the centerpiece of their graduate work, one can easily imagine where it stands among students who have chosen law or business.

At least as measured by the career choices of the graduates interviewed here, the new public service has four other characteristics of note.

The first characteristic is diversity. The new public service is much more diverse than the government-centered public service of old. Traditional demographic indicators show a public service that is becoming more diverse on race and gender and that remains as diverse as ever on intellectual histories. Students are also entering graduate school later and later in career, bringing substantial work experience into the classroom, much of it coming from service in the private and nonprofit sectors. Faculties of the top schools are clearly teaching a very different kind of student today than they did twenty years ago. The average student today is a woman with significant nongovernmental experience and an undergraduate degree in the social sciences (political science or the social sciences more generally).

The second characteristic of the new public service is the rising interest in nongovernmental destinations, particularly in the nonprofit sector. The new public service is much more intentional about going to the nonprofit sector. Not only were recent graduates twice as likely to go nonprofit for first jobs, they appear much more likely to stay in the sector. Recall that only 16 percent of the graduates who went to the nonprofit sector in the 1970s were still there when they were interviewed in 1998. Although it is too early to tell where recent graduates will end up, they appear to have made a much more durable commitment.

The rise of the nonprofit sector as a destination of choice reflects significant changes in what graduates think of the three sectors. Government is seen as the sector most likely to represent the public interest, but trails the private and nonprofit sectors on spending money wisely and helping people. Although where the graduates sit in their current jobs influences what they think of the sectors, there is little doubt that government has lost confidence even among its own recruits. The most significant data point on confidence in government can be found in the bottom left cell of table 3-2 on page 64. Government still ranks among its own as the best place to represent the public interest (73 percent of the combined classes of 1973–74 and 1978–79 who are currently working in government agreed, compared to 68 percent of the combined classes of 1988 and 1993) but has lost significant ground as a place that its own recruits think helps people (43 percent of the classes of 1973–74 and 1978–79 versus 26 percent of the classes of 1988 and 1993). Given the nearly uniform commitment to helping people among these graduates, this is arguably the absolute worst position for government in the competition for talent.

The third characteristic of the new public service is switching. Members of the new public service simply do not stay put. Interestingly, the highest rates of sector switching in this study were found among the earlier classes. These earlier graduates have simply had more time to exercise their choices. But when one controls for the life cycle by asking where graduates went in the first five years after graduation, it seems reasonable to argue that more recent classes will exceed the switching rates of their earlier peers. More recent graduates appear ready and willing to act on their belief that it just is not wise to stay long with any one employer, and they are already outpacing previous classes in changing jobs and sectors in the first five years of career.

The switching rates are not uniform across the three sectors of the new public service, however. Government does not just trail the private and nonprofit sectors in the competition for new graduates, it is also the least likely to hold its talent over time. Regardless of when they went to school, graduates who take their first jobs outside government are more likely to stay put than those who start out inside government.

This is not to argue that the private and nonprofit sectors are particularly effective on their own in holding talent. The nonprofit sector was particularly volatile as a first destination, with significant percentages of graduates moving out over time. But when these graduates left their private or nonprofit jobs, they were significantly more likely to move to another nongovernmental job than into government. Once outside, they were highly likely to stay outside, in part because government offers so few opportunities for entry at the middle and senior levels.

The fourth and final characteristic of the new public service is its deep commitment to making a difference in the world. This is the one characteristic in which the new public service is indistinguishable from the old public service. Graduates in all five classes shared a common motivation to serve and a common concern for finding challenging work and the opportunity to learn. Recruiting a new public servant is still just as simple as it always was: show him or her a good job, with challenge, learning opportunities, a good boss, the chance to make an impact, even a bit of public respect.

It is tempting to describe government's recruitment problems today as little more than a pay problem. After all, the pay problem can be easily solved with more money. The reality is that higher pay might make graduates take a second look, but it will never be enough to make them commit. As the private recruiters who visit the top public policy and administration schools will testify, pay is only tangential to the final choice. That is why private recruiters rarely put a time deadline on their offers. They may show up in October with $65,000 offers and $5,000 signing bonuses, but they know that most public policy and administration graduates wait until they see the range of opportunities before making a final choice. Whether deserved or not, government has a bad reputation as a place to work. And that is a problem that just cannot be solved with higher pay.

Advice to the Profession

The rise of the new public service clearly complicates the education and recruitment process for everyone involved. Students must be more thoughtful as they select courses, graduates must recognize the impact of their first choices, schools must prepare students for highly mobile careers and a volatile job market, government must learn how to compete for talent, and the nonprofit sector and its funders must confront the extraordinary stress reported here.

Beyond these individual responses, everyone also needs to recognize that public service now takes place in many different settings. Much as some readers will object to the private sector as a destination for public service, the reality is that government itself has off-loaded many of its best jobs as it has struggled to meet the downsizing pressure. "Pure types are rare," John D. Donahue writes of the distinction between private and public delivery of service. "In practice, *publicness* and *privateness* are contingent, even slightly artificial categories. 'The Government' is a shorthand term for a collection of people acting within some particular network of rules and expectations. To examine any instance of 'government production' is invariably to discover *people*, variously organized and variously motivated, doing the producing."[1] And, as this study clearly suggests, at least some of those people are coming from the nation's very best schools of public policy and administration. Uncomfortable though it may be to some faculty, more and more students will be heading to the private sector in the future. The challenge is not to stop the trend, but to make sure that each one of those students understands the public obligations of private service.

It is particularly difficult to draw lines between public and private when contractors and civil servants do the same jobs often in the same office at the same time.[2] Much as the size of the paycheck and the level of job security vary, there may be little discernible difference between the management analyst who works for the Commerce Department and the one who works for Arthur Andersen, the computer programmer who works for the Treasury Department and one who works for Unisys, the faculty member who teaches for the Agriculture Department Graduate School and one who teaches for Georgetown University, or the cancer researcher who works for the National Institutes of Health and the one who works for Upjohn. Ultimately, government workers and private contractors can still share a common sense of service. Like identical twins raised apart, they may find themselves working in different sectors at different pay, but can still share an intense commitment to creating public value through their work.[3]

Advice to the Students

Much of the data presented in this study suggests that today's students might be happiest taking courses directly relevant to their preferred destination. After all, where their predecessors sat before graduate school appears to be just as important to views of the sector as where that respondent sits today. Students who arrived in graduate school with government experience were twice as likely to say government did the best job delivering of services on behalf of the public than did students who arrived with nonprofit experience, while students with nonprofit experience were twice as likely to say nonprofits did the best job than were those who arrived with either government or private sector experience.

The temptation to track students by destination is obvious. Why should students headed to the nonprofit sector take classes on government finance when they already know they will be managing a different budget system? Why not just cut them free to specialize? Simply answered, there are three reasons why students should specialize late in their graduate careers, if they choose to specialize by sector at all.

First, graduates who entered the nonprofit sector have had very high switching rates relative to government and the private sector. Although graduates who went to the nonprofit sector and stayed put were very satisfied with their current jobs, the sector had the greatest difficulty in holding onto graduates over time. Unless they are absolutely certain they will never leave the sector, today's students would be well advised to hope for the best (that is, a long career with a well-funded nonprofit agency) and plan for the likely (that is, the same switching career that so many graduates interviewed here reported).

Second, the nonprofit sector is under such great stress relative to government and the private sector that its leaders need every skill they can use and more. Specializing only in techniques relevant to the nonprofit sector may limit a student's ability to bring innovative thinking to a sector in desperate need of change. Even as they move into the advanced courses they need to be successful in their chosen sector, students should be careful not to close out courses that might be helpful in managing the kind of career changes described in this study, particularly given the stresses reported by previous graduates.

Third, none of the sectors exists in a vacuum. Government managers ought to know something about what it is like to work in the nonprofits they fund; nonprofit managers ought to recognize what it is like to work in the private firms against which they compete, and private managers can hardly ignore the practices and policies of the governments they serve. Knowing something about government finance is essential if nonprofits are to secure the funding they need— hence, the value of a course on government grantmaking. So is knowing something about the language of policy analysis, performance management, and quantitative analysis, which is increasingly used to define the scope of work in the sector. Just as a foreign service student headed to China would do well to learn Chinese, a student headed to the nonprofit sector would do well to learn the prevailing languages of government and private finance.

None of this is to argue that students should never specialize. To the contrary, there is plenty of evidence in the analysis of learning gaps to suggest that students headed to the nonprofit sector do need specialized coursework, as do students headed into community economic development, social welfare policy, or government finance. But all students should start by asking themselves some hard questions about their own career plans.

Advice to the Graduates

This study offers a very simple piece of advice to future graduates of the nation's top schools: beware the choice of first job. The pattern could not be clearer: where a graduate starts work has an impact on where that graduate can go in the future. As noted above, graduates who start outside government tend to stay outside. Some stay outside because they become accustomed to the pay, an argument that would likely hold mostly for those who went to the private sector and stayed. Others stay outside because they are drawn to the mission, an argument that would likely hold more for those who went to the nonprofit sector. Still others likely stay out because they have such a negative view of what government can offer by way of opportunities to grow and advance, or because government simply does not offer middle- and upper-level access points.

But whatever the reasons, graduates should understand that starting outside government is more of a life decision than they might suspect. Those who take a private sector job believing that it is merely a short-term compromise needed to cover their debts may be deluding themselves, as are those who take a nonprofit job hoping to move into government later in career once they truly understand how to help people. Although there are opportunities to move back into government in political and exempted positions, these data suggest that the opportunities are limited. Graduates are also well advised to look at the reasons graduates offered in explaining their switch from the outside into government. Whatever government's well-deserved reputation for bureaucracy and frustration, graduates who switched clearly recognized the ability both to make a bigger policy impact and earn greater public respect from the inside.

Even as one encourages graduates to take a second look at government, the data presented in this study also suggest that government is generally the least, not most, satisfying destination for public service professionals. Although the subsample sizes were occasionally small, it appears that the graduates who are happiest in their current jobs are those who went to the nonprofit and stayed or who started out in the private sector and later switched to nonprofit. The data also suggest government does not produce much greater job satisfaction among the graduates it does lure back across the invisible border between the sectors. While acknowledging that this survey did not gauge the level of satisfaction in jobs held immediately before a switch, the graduates who switched to government ranked among the least satisfied with their current work. In fact, there was only one career path that was less satisfying than government work, nonprofit to private. Otherwise, being in government was the least satisfying of all destinations, whether a graduate started and stayed there, or switched over later in career.

There is one other piece of irrefutable advice to graduates in this book. Simply stated, graduates should be open to future learning opportunities. If they are anything like their predecessors, they will leave graduate school very satisfied with their degree and will remain so over their career. But they will also likely sense significant gaps in their training, particularly in maintaining ethical standards and leading others, and these gaps will widen as graduates age into more important work.

This study suggests that their predecessors filled the gaps in several ways. Many returned to graduate school for an additional degree, while others have attended mid-career seminars and workshops of one kind or another. But most of the graduates interviewed here picked up their ethics and leadership skills on the job or from their voluntary engagement with civil society. Although graduate schools can and should do a better job in teaching many of the missing skills identified earlier in this book, there is no course known to educators that can create a core commitment to ethical conduct and public value where none exists beforehand. Just because faith in the possible, trust in others, and an unwavering commitment to honesty are essential for leading public organizations does not mean the nation's top public policy and administration schools are the place to inculcate those core values.[4]

Advice to the Schools

The nation's top schools of public policy and administration can find ample cause for complacency in this study. After all, their graduates report very high satisfaction with the value of their degrees both for their own careers and for students who might follow in their footsteps. Moreover, the graduates seem to be prospering regardless of the career destinations they have chosen. Some are doing remarkably well financially, and the vast majority report high or very high satisfaction in their current jobs.

Nevertheless, if they are not complaining about the quality of their education, these graduates are clearly suggesting that something might be missing in the standard curriculum. Even though the schools can be justifiably pleased with their work, they cannot easily ignore the need for further dialogue about at least four findings in this study. If this book helps to frame that debate, all the better.

First, the schools dare not ignore the remarkable motion embedded in the typical careers of their students. The fact that half of the graduates in this sample had switched sectors at least once in career suggests a need for the kind of career planning that most schools simply do not provide. Search as one might through the catalogues of the top schools, one will find little evidence that the schools are counseling their students on the implications of the key choices described earlier in this chapter. Nor is there much evidence that the schools are providing the kind of ongoing career counseling and training opportunities that their graduates appear to need as they make sector switches. Too many of the top schools stop counseling their students after the first job.

Second, the schools dare not ignore the learning gaps identified in chapter 4. Without suggesting the need for sweeping curricular reform, the survey does encourage at least some soul searching on how the top schools might close at least some of the gaps. Although the schools may well conclude that leading others simply cannot be taught or that ethics is best learned on the job or by example, it will be much more difficult to declare conflict management, managing information and communications technology, and innovation and change as subjects too esoteric to teach. At the very least, the schools might ask why they spend so much time in the core curriculum on subject matter (meaning quantitative methods and policy analysis) that ends in a three-way tie in fifth place on a list of thirteen skills that might be important to their graduates' success. Without arguing that policy analysis should recede in importance as a core requirement in master's degree programs, there is strong evidence here that schools should ask how they might liberate more time for other skills.

Third, even as they examine the relative weight given to quantitative methods and policy analysis in the core curriculum, the schools dare not ignore the different organizational settings that underpin the new public service career. That means teaching students how to detect and manage organizational differences across the sectors. To the extent that graduates are likely to spend their careers either switching sectors or managing the border between government and its private and non-profit partners, organizational diagnosis becomes an essential tool for success. Not only would organizational diagnosis help graduates manage their own careers, it can be considered one component of a rigorous program for teaching students something about leading others.

Fourth, the schools dare not ignore the clear intentions of students who are headed into the nonprofit sector. Even as students should take care not to narrow their coursework prematurely, the top schools should make sure that they provide meaningful coursework on the nonprofit sector, lest they lose those students to business, education, and social work schools, which are now competing for a share of this growing market. Merely renaming courses on financial or public management to include nonprofits is not enough.

Even as they review their programs in isolation, the nation's leading schools of public policy and administration must ask whether they should join together to take a more visible position on the current state of the public service, for example, through their two trade associations, the National Association of Schools of Public Affairs and Administration and the Association for Public Policy Analysis and Management, or through a special task force or commission. The schools have yet to rise as a collective voice of the profession, whether on how government and the nonprofit sector might improve the hiring and career development process or on how government might structure the procurement process to create opportunities for crossovers from the private sector into government. Where the schools have entered the policy debate, it has largely been through the actions of individual deans and professors. This study suggests that it may be time for a more activist, unified stance.

Advice to the Government

Governments at all levels of the American system face an enormous challenge in competing for their share of talent in the new public service. They are simply not offering enough of the work that graduates of the top schools want. As already noted, higher entry-level pay might make those graduates take another look at government as an option but cannot make government more competitive on its own. Nor will a more aggressive recruiting process. Although better advertising and an occasional appearance on campus by cabinet members would give government a higher profile in the annual recruiting competition, graduates of the top schools are not likely to be swayed unless government can deliver what they want.

The message to government recruiters from these graduates is simple. Offer a good job with room to grow and advance, and recruitment and retention will be easy. Offer dead-end jobs in towering bureaucracies, with no funding for training, no hope of good work, and no chance to rise, and new recruits will leave at the first chance. Unfortunately, at least at the leading schools, government often offers no job at all. But for the federal Presidential Management Internship, it is still up to the students to find government, not vice versa.

This is not the place to make the case for flatter, more agile government, although that case can clearly be made; nor is it the place to argue for broader career paths or even restoration of the rotational assignments that once made the Presidential Management Internships one of the most exciting learning opportunities in government, although that case can be well made, too. Suffice it to note that governments at all levels have neglected the career development process for decades, allowing individual departments and agencies to ignore the steady calcification of career paths and erosion of learning opportunities.

Even where there have been reform efforts, implementation has been weak at best, hostile at worst. At the federal level, for example, the twentieth anniversary of the 1978 federal Civil Service Reform Act was more a cause for black crepe than celebration, its plans for pay for performance an acknowledged failure, its design for an elite, highly mobile Senior Executive Service an insular disappointment, its invitation to experimentation mostly forgotten in a series of tiny initiatives, and its grand inventory of new opportunities for learning and growth a distant, unfunded mirage. State and local government have hardly done better. With notable exceptions in states such as Minnesota, South Carolina, and Georgia, and cities such as Indianapolis, government hierarchies continue to thicken, while outsourcing fever continues to rise.

None of this is to argue that government is a vast desert of dead-end work. There are still good jobs in government, even if they are often the best kept secrets in the labor market. Rather, it is to confirm that many of the nation's most talented public servants increasingly believe that good jobs in government are the exception, not the rule. It is a belief that extends well beyond the professionals interviewed for this study. As I have argued elsewhere, the good news is that young Americans generally believe that government is a good place to work, but the bad news is that they believe it is a good place for almost anyone *but* them. Moreover, roughly half of those who say they might like to work for government list pay, benefits, and security as their prime motivations, hardly the kind of public service ethic that government should seek.[5]

The question is what government can do to become more competitive. The first step is to declare a human capital crisis in government. Simply stated, the government talent pool is draining out with less and less in the pipeline to replace it. It is a crisis of staggering importance, and one that merits immediate action among legislators and executives alike. It is also a problem that cannot be solved with the current inventory of government recruitment programs, most of which were designed for a work force that has not existed in years. Even as government makes it easy for its most talented employees to exit at any point in career, it is doing virtually nothing to create new entry points for replacements to enter later in career. Unfortunately, legislators and executives have shown little interest in addressing the crisis, perhaps because they have been spending so much time cutting government and imposing head count constraints.

The second step is to recognize that recruitment and retention are no longer two sides of the same coin. Simply stated, government must become more aggressive at middle- and upper-level recruiting, which means that it must open more jobs to competition from the outside. Instead of reserving the vast majority of promotions for internal candidates, government must open the career path to outside competition. There is no doubt that some talented employees will leave government, but the departures may be a small price to pay to gain access to the talented outsiders who might answer the call. Assuming that the graduates interviewed for this study are reasonably representative of the public service in general, there appears to be a significant reservoir of interest in government jobs later in career. The vast majority of graduates still believe that working for government is part of a public service career, even graduates who have spent their careers thus far working solely outside of government.

For the time being, however, the path into government at mid-career is difficult at best, nearly impenetrable at worst. Middle-level jobs are rarely advertised broadly, and recruitment incentives are nonexistent. The challenge here is not to shame graduates for taking first jobs in the private or nonprofit sectors, therefore, but to convince governments at all levels to design personnel systems that might some-day lure a high-flier for a stop in government, however long or short, along his or her career.

The third step is to recognize that recruitment does not end with the formal hiring process. Government has an obligation to provide challenging work and the opportunity for growth, as do private firms and nonprofit agencies. Given the difficulties in attracting talented cit-izens to the public service in a red-hot labor market, it behooves all three sectors to give their employees a chance to make an impact, even if they well know those employees will someday leave for another sec-tor. Even as they compete against each other for talent, the three sec-tors are also competing against the rest of the economy for talent.

Ultimately, there is nothing more irresponsible than to squander this scarce talent in dead-end jobs. That means paying attention to career development and job enrichment as an ongoing organizational obliga-tion, wherever the organization exists. The problem for government is that it has lost much of the expertise to design the kind of recruitment, retention, and career development options that might attract a fair share of the top graduates. Thus, the place to increase government's competitive edge may well be in rebuilding its human resource offices, which have been decimated by a decade of downsizing. Most govern-ment agencies are barely able to keep their hiring processes moving, let alone design alternative career paths and job enrichment programs for a new public service. Being a human resource officer in government has become one of the worst jobs in the labor market, one marked by high stress and limited opportunity to make a difference.

Rebuilding the human resource profession cannot change the state of the government service on its own, however. Legislators and exec-utives at all levels of government must also recognize the need for rad-ical change in how their agencies recruit and develop talent. As long as the nation's political leaders see civil service reform as the policy issue of last resort, ignore it in their annual state of the union, state of the state, and state of the city addresses, and underfund it in the budget, government's human capital will continue to decay. And that means acting on it more than once every twenty years.

Advice to the Nonprofit Sector and Its Funders

This study offers a mixed portrait of the nonprofit sector as a destination for service. On the one hand, graduates who went to the nonprofit sector for first jobs or on switches were the most satisfied of any graduates. On the other hand, they report significant stress in their work and were also the most likely to leave at some point in career. Recall that just 46 percent of the graduates who started out in the nonprofit sector were still there at the time of this study, compared to 57 percent of those who started in government and 55 percent of those who started in the private sector.

The explanations for this mixed portrait are hardly surprising for those who care about the sector. As the in-depth interviews with the classes of 1988 and 1993 clearly suggest, the nonprofit sector is a destination filled with both great meaning and intense stress. The sector is doing well on recruitment but courting disaster on retention.

It is not clear how the nonprofit sector can endure the kind of leadership turnover indicated here. Unlike government, which has always had more than enough managers to fill any middle- or upper-level opening, or the private sector, which has always had enough money to skim the cream for the talent it needs from other sectors, nonprofit agencies are notoriously flat organizations. Without painting the entire sector with a broad brush, it seems reasonable to suggest that funders pay increased attention to the nonprofit talent pool. Whatever the line of work, if nonprofits are to survive and flourish in the current environment of tight budgets and increased competition, they must have a stable corps of talented leaders.

The problem in the sector is that many funders seem unwilling to invest in the leadership capacity of the organizations they fund. To the contrary, foundations seem to be less and less willing to fund the ancillary activities that might help a nonprofit retain its talent over time, even as their grants fuel extraordinary growth in the sheer number of nonprofits competing for resources. Without saying that the sector is in desperate need of drastic reshaping, it does need to take stock of its current human capital and ask whether and how it can strengthen retention in the future. Absent intervention, the ultimate victor in the talent wars of the future is likely to be the private sector, not government.

It would be ridiculous to argue that foundations may someday find themselves without enough nonprofits to fund. After all, there will always be think tanks and universities to support. However, there is ample evidence here that they may someday find themselves without enough talented nonprofits to produce the results they desire. The combination of continued expansion in the absolute number of non-profits and the turnover rates described above suggest an emerging crisis of capacity that funders would do well to address now rather than later. The sector still retains an enormous advantage in recruit-ment, but it has much to do to increase the odds that its talent will stay put.

Advice to the Private Sector

This study clearly suggests that the private sector has already mas-tered many of the lessons for recruiting talented employees. Make the offer early, talk about career paths, provide meaningful work, give graduates a sense of purpose, and pay a high premium. But for the subtle bias toward government and nonprofit work at most of the nation's top public policy and administration schools, one suspects that the private sector would have drawn an even higher share of the graduates.

If there is a single recommendation that comes from this study, it is that the private sector embrace its responsibility to shepherd the tal-ent it recruits away from the other two sectors. Bluntly put, there are too many private contractors that view their public policy and admin-istration graduates as mere fodder for fueling their burgeoning gov-ernment practices. If their employees wash out after a few years of intense but highly paid work, that is merely a cost of doing business.

The private sector also needs to confront its reputation among these graduates as a destination with little opportunity for impact and mini-mal public respect. The answer may be in a more visible embrace of the public obligations of private service. The Rockwell employees who bolt the Space Shuttle hatch are no less obligated to do the job properly than are the NASA employees who work at their side; the Lockheed Martin employees who administer state welfare programs are no less obligated to be fair and accurate than are the employees they replace; the ICF-Kaiser employees who meet with concerned citizens at Superfund sites are no less obligated to be responsive than are the Environmental Protection Agency employees they represent; the Westinghouse employees who clean up nuclear waste sites are no less obligated to protect public safety than are the Department of Energy employees who guide their contracts. The more government relies on third parties to deliver public services once delivered in-house, the more those third parties must recognize the public obligations of their service.

Luckily, they can make those obligations visible in many ways, whether by celebrating the public service that they provide, supporting efforts to strengthen government's human capital through their lobbying activities, or encouraging their senior executives to accept political appointments in government.[6] For the time being, however, the relationship is too often one-way only: the private sector skims the cream of the talent, leaving government and the nonprofit sector scrambling for what remains. It is no surprise, therefore, that so many of the graduates did not see the private sector as a respected destination. The sector itself does not acknowledge its role in the public service either.

One final word of advice to the private sector is warranted. Even as it competes against government for talent, the private sector needs to support efforts to improve government's competitiveness against the private sector. Private firms have just as much at stake in helping government recruit talented employees as have any other citzens.

Conclusion

It is difficult to conclude a study that has as many findings, positive and negative, as this one does. On the one hand, there is ample cause for concern in these pages, particularly in the movement away from government within the new public service. It is not at all clear how government can be well executed unless it is able to compete more effectively for its fair share of talent. On the other hand, there is ample cause for pride in the graduates who occupy the new public service, and good reason to congratulate their schools for giving their students many of the skills needed to succeed in multisectored careers.

Perhaps the best way to conclude this study is to note that the vast majority of these new public servants would do it all over again. Asked whether they would like to see their sons and daughters pursue a career in public service, almost 70 percent of the graduates answered yes, with well over two thirds of that number answering yes strongly.

As with so much in this study, there were slight variations here and there. Graduates working in the nonprofit sector at the time of the survey were once again the most enthusiastic about public service: 53 percent gave a strong yes to the question, compared to 48 percent and 44 percent respectively of the graduates working in government and the private sector. At the same time, members of earlier classes were somewhat less enthusiastic about the public service than more recent classes: 23 percent of the classes of 1973 and 1974 answered no to the question, compared to 14 percent of the class of 1993.

Nevertheless, the general results suggest significant satisfaction, indeed hopefulness, among the graduates with the lives that they have chosen, and a general sense of service that anchors the profession across the sectors that now produce goods and services on the public's behalf. Although there is certainly cause for concern embedded in some of the findings discussed above, anyone who cares about the future of public service can find great hope in this research. These graduates are deeply committed to making a difference in their world and ask only that their employers take that commitment seriously enough to provide challenging work and the opportunity to grow. And that is really not much to ask, given the depth of their willingness to serve.

Ultimately, this is a profession of which the nation's leading schools, indeed the nation as a whole, can be justifiably proud. They have embraced sweeping changes in the labor market with aplomb, all the while maintaining the core commitment to the public service ethic that brought them to graduate school in the first place. Although many are still searching for the right job, at least they are searching with the right compass. And that is very good news for the future of the new public service.

SURVEY METHODOLOGY

The survey on which this book is based was conducted by Princeton Survey Research Associates, Inc., and involved a sample of exactly 1,000 persons living in the continental United States who received a master's degree in public policy, public administration, or public affairs from one of thirteen top-ranked programs described below. The sample was selected using five graduating class cohorts: 1973 and 1974, 1978 and 1979, 1983, 1988, and 1993. The interviews were conducted from September 22 through November 7, 1998.

Sample Design

Princeton Survey Research Associates used *U.S. News and World Report*'s 1998 ranking of the top twenty graduate programs in public policy, public administration, and public affairs to select schools. Thirteen of the top twenty programs agreed to participate by providing alumni lists with contact information.

This technical appendix was drafted by the research staff at Princeton Survey Research Associates, Inc., and edited by the author.

The sample for this survey was designed to produce a representative sample of graduates by three kinds of master's programs: comprehensive, policy analysis, and public administration. Table A-1 provides details on the selected schools by program type, as well as information on the degrees offered by each institution. Alumni directories and databases supplied by selected schools were used to build the sampling frame. Contact information provided varied from school to school, but all sampled cases included name, home telephone number, degree obtained, and year graduated. Although some alumni directories included business contacts, only two percent of respondents were reached through business contact information. It is important to note that the alumni directories may not have included all graduates of a given class. Table A-2 provides information on the type of contact information available in the directories and databases provided by each school.

The sample was selected to be proportionate across the three strata of program types. Table A-3 provides sample sizes by school, graduation year, and program type.

Interview Completion Procedures

At least twenty attempts were made to complete an interview with every sampled graduate. Calls were staggered over time of day and day of the week to maximize the chances of making contact with each graduate. All respondents who refused an interview or stopped an interview in midstream were recontacted at least once in an attempt to convince them to complete interviews.

If a contact resulted in an answering machine or voice messaging service, the interviewer left the following message to encourage participation:

Hello, my name is _____ and I'm calling from Princeton Survey Research Associates. We're conducting a survey of people who have master's degrees in public affairs, public policy, and public administration. We're interviewing professionals nationwide who have degrees from the top master's programs about career and life-style issues. Please call us toll free at [number given] to participate in this survey.

Table A-1. Sample Schools, by Program Type

Program type	School	Degrees offered[a]
Comprehensive	Harvard University	MPA, MPP
	University of Indiana	MPA
	University of Minnesota	MPAF
	University of North Carolina	MPA
	Syracuse University	MPA, MA
	University of Texas	MPAF
	University of Washington	MPAF
Policy analysis	Carnegie Mellon University	MPM, MS
	University of Chicago	MPP
	University of Michigan	MPA
Public administration	University of Kansas	MPA
	State University of New York, Albany	MPA
	University of Southern California	MPA, MPP

a. MA = Master of Arts; MPA = Master of Public Administration (all Harvard MPAs represent mid-career degrees); MPAF = Master of Public Affairs; MPM = Master of Public Policy and Management (Carnegie Mellon only); MPP = Master of Public Policy; MS = Master of Science in Public Management (mid-career degree, Carnegie Mellon only).

Table A-2. Type of Contact Information Available, by Program Type and School

Program type and school	Contact information provided
Comprehensive programs	
Harvard University	Home and business (in most cases)
University of Indiana	Home only
University of Minnesota	Home and business (in most cases)
University of North Carolina	Home and business (in most cases)
Syracuse University	Predominately home (with few business exceptions)
University of Texas	Home and business (in most cases)
University of Washington	Home and business (in most cases)
Policy analysis programs	
Carnegie Mellon University	Home and business (in most cases)
University of Chicago	Predominately home (with few business exceptions)
University of Michigan	Home and business (in most cases)
Public administration programs	
University of Kansas	Home and business (in most cases)
State University of New York, Albany	Predominately home (with few business exceptions)
University of Southern California	Predominately home (with few business exceptions)

Table A-3. Sample Sizes by Program Type, School, and Graduation Year

| Program type and school | Graduation year | | | | | |
	1973–74	1978–79	1983	1988	1993	Total
Comprehensive programs						
Harvard	87	126	138	223	196	770
Indiana	39	47	31	24	52	193
Minnesota	31	58	25	42	53	209
University of North Carolina	26	26[a]	17	24	15	108
Syracuse	109	132	43	33	41	358
Texas	56	104	74	59	66	359
Washington	61	71	46	25	35	238
Total						2,235
Policy analysis programs						
Carnegie Mellon	.12[b]	30[a]	32	120	138	332
Chicago	0	0	11	18	15	44
Michigan	36	42	26	25	44	173
Total						549
Public administration programs						
Kansas	17	20	9	13	14	73
State University of New York, Albany	104	101	30	39	41	315
University of Southern California	109[b]	147[a]	54	37	30	377
Total						765

a. Only 1978 graduates included.
b. Only 1973 graduates included.

Approximately one-third of the graduates who heard this message returned the call and completed an interview.

The accuracy of the contact information provided by the alumni directories obviously varied. If a contact number was found to be not working, continuously ringing but never answered, busy, a computer or fax tone, or a government or business number (but not the graduate's business number), or if a household was contacted in which the selected graduate did not live or a language problem existed, other contact information for the graduate was used to find a new telephone number. Four hundred and seventy-eight graduates had problem telephone numbers, and new telephone numbers were found for 303 of those. The vast majority of the telephone number problems were due to typographical errors in the alumni directories, and an additional 10 percent of the problems were due to area code changes. Approximately 15 percent were entirely new telephone numbers. Approximately 200 of the 303 new telephone numbers resulted in completed interviews.

The final survey was based on completed interviews with 1,000 respondents drawn from the 3,549 names in the original sample. The distribution of those 3,549 telephone numbers is described below:

Nonsample numbers
Telephone number not in service	744
Business, fax, or modem number	197
Total	941

Potential nonsample numbers
Telephone rings but is not answered	119
Busy signal	30
Incomplete information	35
Total	184

Numbers with unknown eligibility
Call back another time	216
Answering machine answers	241
Total	457

Numbers with no eligible graduate
Language barrier	15
Graduate not in household	415
Individual did not receive master's degree	44
Total	474

Numbers with eligible graduate
Incomplete interviews	16
Complete interviews	1,000
Graduates who refused an interview	477
Total	1,493
Total telephone numbers	3,549

Of the graduates in the sample, 74.4 percent were contacted by an interviewer and 77.0 percent agreed to cooperate. Sixty-nine percent were found eligible for the interview. Furthermore, 98.4 percent of eligible respondents completed the interview. Therefore, the final response rate is 56.4 percent (the product of the 74.4 percent contact rate, the 77.0 percent cooperation rate, and the 98.4 percent completion rate).

SURVEY QUESTIONNAIRE

Q1.   After college some people work for a while before getting a master's degree, while others go straight to graduate school. Did you work before entering your master's program in [*insert degree*]?

Percent
 69 Worked
 31 Went right to graduate school

Percent
 * Don't know
 0 Refused

Ask Q2–Q3 if worked before graduate program [Q1 = 1]:

Q2.   About how many years did you work before entering your master's program? (N = 689)

Percent
 48 Less than five years
 31 Five to ten years
 20 Greater than ten years

Percent
 * Don't know
 0 Refused

Q3.   Thinking about the jobs you held before your master's program, did you spend most of your time working for government, private companies, or nonprofit groups? (N = 689)

Percent
 48 Government
 27 Private companies
 22 Nonprofit groups

Percent
 2 Other
 * Don't know
 1 Refused

Ask if worked for government before Master's program [Q3 = 1]:

Q4. Was that federal, state, or local government [*multiple responses accepted*]? (*N* = 332)

Percent		Percent	
42	Federal	3	Other
34	State	1	Don't know
26	Local	1	Refused

Q5. A. And, are you currently employed full-time, part-time or are you not employed?

Percent		Percent	
81	Full-time	*	Don't know
7	Part-time	*	Refused
11	Not employed		

B. Since you got your master's, how many different places have you worked—one, two, or three or more places?

Percent		Percent	
23	None	26	Three or more
28	One	0	Don't know
23	Two	0	Refused

Q6–Q7 Thinking about (the [first | next] place you worked after your master's program . . . /your current place of employment . . .)

A. Was/Is your employer government, a private company, or a nonprofit group?

Percent

	First job	Second job	Third job	Fourth job	Current job
Government	62	44	41	35	45
Private company	19	31	40	40	31
Nonprofit group	18	23	17	21	19
Self-employed	1	2	1	3	4
Other	*	0	1	0	*
Don't know	*	*	*	0	0
Refused	0	1	*	1	1
N =	770	489	263	124	884

If in government:

B. Federal, state, or local government?

Percent

	First job	Second job	Third job	Fourth job	Current job
Federal	28	27	26	26	29
State	40	35	37	44	42
Local	29	35	36	26	27
Other	2	1	0	2	2
Don't know	0	*	0	0	0
Refused	1	1	0	2	0
N =	477	213	107	43	400

If not in government:

C. *If not self-employed:* (Did | does) this employer receive any government funds for the work it did /*If self-employed:* (Did | does) your organization receive any government funds for the work you did—for example, through government contracts or grants?

Percent

	First job	Second job	Third job	Fourth job	Current job
Yes	46	47	34	36	47
No	51	51	63	63	50
Don't know	3	1	2	0	1
Refused	0	0	1	1	1
N =	293	276	156	81	484

If employer (received | receives) government funds:

D. On average, what percentage of the time did you personally spend working on projects funded by the government?

Percent

	First job	Second job	Third job	Fourth job	Current job
20% of the time or less	22	29	30	38	39
21% to 80% of the time	28	28	25	21	28
Greater than 80% of the time	44	37	38	41	28
Don't know	6	5	6	0	4
Refused	0	0	2	0	1
N =	135	131	53	29	226

E. *If not self-employed:* How many years (did I have) you (work I worked) for this employer? /*If self-employed:* How many years were you/have you been self-employed?)

Percent

	First job	Second job	Third job	Fourth job	Current job
One year or less	27	26	22	19	16
2–3 years	32	38	41	31	19
4–5 years	15	16	18	25	14
6–10 years	14	13	13	19	18
More than 10 years	12	7	5	5	31
Don't know	0	*	1	0	*
Refused	*	0	*	1	1
N =	770	489	263	124	884

If not self-employed:

F. And, how many different positions did you hold with this employer?

Percent

	First job	Second job	Third job	Fourth job	Current job
One position	56	68	72	73	49
Two positions	20	21	17	15	19
Three positions	13	6	7	8	15
More than three	10	4	4	3	17
Don't know	*	0	*	0	*
Refused	0	0	*	1	1
N =	766	479	260	120	853

G. All things considered, (were I are) you very satisfied, somewhat satisfied, somewhat dissatisfied, or very dissatisfied (*if not self-employed:* working for this employer/*if self-employed:* with this working situation)?

Percent

	First job	Second job	Third job	Fourth job	Current job
Very satisfied	49	51	48	60	67
Somewhat satisfied	37	35	36	24	25
Somewhat dissatisfied	8	10	10	9	5
Very dissatisfied	6	4	5	6	1
Don't know	*	*	*	0	*
Refused	0	*	*	1	1
N =	770	489	263	124	884

H. Do you consider the work you did (*if not self-employed:* for this employer/*if self-employed:* when you were self employed) a form of "public service," or not?

Percent

	First job	Second job	Third job	Fourth job	Current job
Yes, was "public service"	82	75	67	69	76
No was not	18	25	32	31	23
Don't know	*	0	*	0	*
Refused	*	*	1	1	1
N =	770	489	263	124	884

Ask if considers current job public service [Q7H = 1]

Q8. You said you consider your current work a form of public service, would you please describe the "public service" aspects of your work? (*N* = 670)

Percent
- 10 Education
- 12 Public assistance/social services
- 4 Law/criminal justice
- 6 Medical/health care
- 13 Government
- 3 Public works/utilities/ transportation
- 3 Environment
- 10 Banking/finance/economic development

Percent
- 1 Writer/journalist
- 11 Information provider/analyst/ research
- 1 Mediator
- 2 Foreign/overseas
- 10 Other
- 1 Don't know
- 12 Refused

Ask if ever employed since master's program [Q5B = 2–4]
(N = 992):

Q11. There are many different factors that someone might consider when choosing whether or not to accept a position with an employer. Thinking back to your decision to take your first position after your master's program, (was I were) the [*insert item—do not rotate*] a very important consideration, somewhat important, not too important, or not a consideration at all in your decision to take that position?

Percent

	Very important	Somewhat important	Not too important	Not important	Don't know	Refused
a. Salary	17	47	23	12	*	1
b. Benefits	25	36	24	13	*	1
c. Job security	21	28	31	19	*	1
d. Opportunity for advancement	47	27	15	10	*	1
e. Opportunity for personal growth and skill development	75	18	3	2	*	1
f. Public respect for the type of work you'd be doing	41	36	14	7	*	1
g. Opportunity to impact local or national issues	52	25	14	8	*	1
h. Type of work involved	70	22	5	2	*	1
i. Opportunity to do challenging work	80	15	3	2	0	1

Ask if switched job sectors at least once. Ask about the first time respondent made such a switch.

Q12.   Earlier you said that you first worked in (government I a private company I the non profit sector) after your master's program, but you later changed jobs to work for (government I a private company I a nonprofit group). Thinking back to your decision to enter (government I a private company I the nonprofit sector) after working in (government I a private company I a nonprofit group), (was I were) the [*insert item—do not rotate*] a very important consideration, somewhat important, not too important, or not a consideration at all in your decision to make this move?

Switched from government to private/nonprofit sector (*N* = 259):

Percent

	Very important	Somewhat important	Not too important	Not important	Don't know	Refused
a. Salary	27	33	22	15	0	3
b. Benefits	23	27	25	22	*	3
c. Job security	17	24	31	24	1	3
d. Opportunity for advancement	42	25	13	16	0	3
e. Opportunity for personal growth and skill development	75	14	2	5	0	3
f. Public respect for the type of work you'd be doing	35	30	15	16	*	3
g. Opportunity to impact local or national issues	39	18	19	20	*	3
h. Type of work involved	64	22	7	4	0	3
i. Opportunity to do challenging work	73	17	3	4	0	3

Switched from private/nonprofit sector to government ($N = 101$):

Percent

	Very important	Somewhat important	Not too important	Not important	Don't know	Refused
a. Salary	17	46	19	14	1	4
b. Benefits	24	37	24	11	1	4
c. Job Security	19	26	37	14	1	4
d. Opportunity for advancement	36	34	17	9	1	4
e. Opportunity for personal growth and skill development	68	22	3	1	1	5
f. Public respect for the type of work you'd be doing	50	28	11	5	1	5
g. Opportunity to impact local or national issues	58	24	8	5	0	5
h. Type of work involved	66	24	1	2	1	6
i. Opportunity to do challenging work	69	24	1	1	1	4

Ask Q13–Q14 if currently employed [Q5A = 1,2] (N = 884)

Q13. Thinking now about your decision to take a position with your current employer/(*if self-employed:* go into business for yourself), (was I were) the following a very important consideration, somewhat important, not too important, or not a consideration at all in your decision to take a position with the employer?/(*if self-employed:* go into business for yourself)?

Percent

	Very important	Somewhat important	Not too important	Not important	Don't know	Refused
a. Salary	38	41	12	8	*	1
b. Benefits	43	34	13	9	*	1
c. Job security	38	31	19	11	*	2
d. Opportunity for advancement	48	29	13	9	*	1
e. Opportunity for personal growth and skill development	72	18	5	3	*	1
f. Public respect for the type of work you'd be doing	48	30	13	7	*	1
g. Opportunity to impact local or national issues	54	23	13	9	*	1
h. Type of work involved	71	22	3	2	*	2
i. Opportunity to do challenging work	77	17	4	2	*	1

Q14. Do you think you'll stay in (government I private business I the nonprofit sector) for the rest of your career, or do you think you'll switch sectors (again) at some point? (*N = 884*)

Percent
46 Stay in the same sector
39 Switch sectors

Percent
14 Don't know
 1 Refused

If plan to stay in same sector [Q14 = 1]:

Q15.   And do you think you'll stay with your current employer/(*if self-employed:* remain self-employed) for the rest of your career, or do you think you'll switch employers? (*N* = 410)

Percent		Percent	
58	Stay with the same employer	9	Don't know
32	Switch employers	1	Refused

Ask Q16 if switched job sectors at least once.

Q16.   You mentioned that you left a (government | private sector | nonprofit) job for one in (the private sector | a nonprofit organization | government). In your own words, what is the main reason you made that move?

Percent

	Switched from government to private	Switched from private or nonprofit to government
Career opportunities/better job	14	24
Frustration/bored/needed a change	12	20
Money/salary/security	12	5
Retired/laid off/job ended	6	0
Flexibility/time with family	8	3
Ability to make impact	7	8
Have own business	5	0
To move/relocate/didn't like area	5	0
More education	6	0
Other	13	26
Don't know	1	2
Refused	12	13
N =	259	101

Ask Q17 if ever employed since master's program [Q5B = 2–4]:

Q17.   In the course of your career, how many times, if at all, have you and those you worked with been required to change how you work as a result of a reform effort such as "reinventing" or "total quality management?" (N = 992)

Percent		Percent	
39	0 times	18	4 or more times
16	1 time	5	Don't know
21	2 or 3 times	1	Refused

Ask Q18 if ever employed since master's program [Q17 = 1–97]:

Q18.   In your experience have these reform efforts generally made things much better in your workplace, somewhat better, somewhat worse, much worse, or haven't they made any difference one way or the other? (N = 544)

Percent		Percent	
15	Much better	3	Don't know
39	Somewhat better	*	Refused
13	Somewhat worse		
3	Much worse		
27	Haven't made any difference one way or the other		

Q19.   On average, about how many years do you think a person should stay with any given employer before moving on?

Percent		Percent	
27	Less than five years	36	Don't know
30	Five to ten years	2	Refused
5	Greater than ten years		

Q20.   And, in the course of a public service career, about how long do you think a person should work in government?

Percent
15   Less than five years
24   Five to ten years
18   Greater than ten years

Percent
42   Don't know
2   Refused

Q21.   In general, if you could choose, would you rather work for government, private business, or a nonprofit organization? Do you feel strongly about that or not?

Percent
38   Government
31   Strongly
7   Not strongly
24   Private business
18   Strongly
6   Not strongly

Percent
25   Nonprofit
17   Strongly
8   Not strongly
11   Don't know
2   Refused

Q22.   If you had a son or daughter just getting out of school, would you like to see him or her pursue a career in public service or not? Do you feel strongly about that or not?

Percent
68   Yes
48   Strongly
20   Not strongly
21   No
12   Strongly
9   Not strongly

Percent
10   Don't know
1   Refused

Q23.   Next, thinking about your master's degree program, how well did it prepare you for the different jobs you have had—very well, somewhat well, not too well, or not well at all?

Percent
47   Very well
42   Somewhat well
7   Not too well

Percent
3   Not well at all
1   Don't know
*   Refused

Q24. Now, imagine someone starting a career today with the exact training you received in your master's program. How prepared would this person be for a career in public service? Would they be very well prepared, somewhat well, not too well, or not well prepared at all for a career in public service?

Percent		Percent	
43	Very well	3	Not well at all
44	Somewhat well	3	Don't know
7	Not too well	*	Refused

Q25. Thinking about the different skills needed to achieve job success, how important have each of the following been in your job success. . . ?

Percent

	Very important	Somewhat important	Not too important	Not important	Don't know	Refused
a. Managing conflict	62	29	7	1	1	*
b. Managing a diverse work force	43	35	14	7	*	*
c. Writing regulations and legislation	28	28	24	19	1	*
d. Doing policy analysis	55	29	10	6	1	*
e. Budgeting and public finance	51	29	12	7	1	*
f. Managing innovation and change	55	32	8	3	1	*
g. Analyzing and influencing public opinion	37	36	17	8	1	*
h. Managing media relations	29	34	25	12	1	*
i. Raising money and generating extra revenue	30	24	24	20	1	*
j. Influencing policymakers	55	31	8	5	1	*
k. Leading others	72	23	4	2	*	*
l. Maintaining ethical standards	82	14	2	2	*	*
m. Managing information and communication technology	56	32	9	4	*	*

Q26.   (Next) how helpful was your master's program in teaching you about [*insert item—do not rotate*] . . . was your graduate program very helpful, somewhat helpful, not too helpful, or not helpful at all?

Percent

		Very important	Somewhat important	Not too important	Not important	Don't know	Refused
a.	Managing conflict	28	37	22	12	1	*
b.	Managing a diverse work force	22	32	27	18	1	*
c.	Writing regulations and legislation	26	37	20	14	3	1
d.	Doing policy analysis	65	27	4	3	1	*
e.	Budgeting and public finance	48	37	9	4	1	*
f.	Managing innovation and change	33	40	18	8	1	*
g.	Analyzing and influencing public opinion	32	40	17	9	2	*
h.	Managing media relations	17	29	29	23	2	*
i.	Raising money and generating extra revenue	15	20	33	31	1	1
j.	Influencing policymakers	41	44	8	6	1	*
k.	Leading others	40	43	11	6	1	*
l.	Maintaining ethical standards	48	38	9	5	1	*
m.	Managing information and communication technology	27	34	22	15	1	*

Q27.   All in all, how much of the time do you think you can trust [*insert item—rotate*] to do what is right? Just about always, most of the time, or only some of the time?

Percent

	Just about always	Most of the time	Only some of the time	Never	Don't know	refused
a. The federal government in Washington	8	37	49	4	2	*
b. Your state government	9	42	44	3	1	1
c. Your local government	12	46	37	3	1	1
d. Private business	8	36	50	4	2	1
e. Nonprofit organizations	14	54	28	1	2	1
f. Charitable organizations	13	57	25	1	3	1
g. The organization or firm you work for	32	46	18	1	2	1

Q28.   In general, who do you trust more to do the right thing? The elected officials who lead the federal government or the civil service employees who run federal government departments and agencies?

Percent
15 Elected officials
62 Civil service employees
16 Both equally/neither

Percent
7 Don't know
1 Refused

Q29.   Who do you have the most confidence in to deliver services on the public's behalf—government, private contractors, or nonprofit organizations?

Percent
42 Government
17 Private contractors
29 Nonprofit organizations

Percent
6 All/none
6 Don't know
1 Refused

Q30. More specifically, who does the best job of [*insert item: rotate*]—government, private contractors, or nonprofit organizations?

Percent

	Govt.	Private	Non-profit	All/none	Don't know	Refused
a. Spending money wisely	15	38	33	7	6	1
b. Representing the public interest	59	5	26	5	5	1
c. Helping people	30	6	52	6	5	1

Demographics

D1. Respondent's sex

Percent
61 Male

Percent
39 Female

D2. What was your undergraduate major?

Percent
7 Business
23 Humanities
30 Government
14 Sciences

Percent
22 Social sciences
2 Other
1 Don't know
9 Refused

D3. A. Since getting your master's degree, have you worked toward any other degrees?

Percent
25 Yes
75 No

Percent
0 Don't know
* Refused

B. What degree, or degrees, have you worked toward? (*N* = 250)

Percent
31 Ph.D.
29 Master's
16 Law

Percent
4 Other
20 Degree unknown

C. Did you receive this/these degrees? ($N = 250$)

Percent
  69 Yes, all
  10 Yes, some

Percent
  21 No, none

D4/5. In politics today, do you consider yourself a Republican, Democrat, or Independent?

Percent
  18 Republican
  49 Democrat
     33 Independent/other/refused
      8 Lean Republican
     11 Lean Democrat
     14 Lean neither/don't know/refused

Percent
  61 Total Democrat
  25 Total Republican

D6. In general, would you describe your political views as very liberal, liberal, moderate, conservative, or very conservative?

Percent
  11 Very liberal
  25 Liberal
  47 Moderate
  12 Conservative

Percent
  2 Very conservative
  1 Don't know
  2 Refused

D7. What is your age?

Percent
  16 Under 35
  33 35 to under 45
  50 45 and over

Percent
  * Don't know
  2 Refused

D8. Last year, that is in 1997, what was your total personal income from all sources, before taxes? Just stop me when I get to the right category [read].

Percent		Percent	
3	Less than $10,000	17	75,000 to under 100,000
1	10,000 to under 20,000		
4	20,000 to under 30,000	18	100,000 or more
14	30,000 to under 50,000	1	Don't know
25	50,000 to under 75,000	16	Refused

D9. Are you, yourself, of Hispanic or Latino background, such as Mexican, Puerto Rican, Cuban, or some other Spanish background?

Percent		Percent	
4	Yes	*	Don't know
94	No	2	Refused

D10. What is your race? Are you white, black or African American, Asian, or some other race?

Percent		Percent	
88	White	2	Other or mixed race
5	Black	0	Don't know
2	Asian	2	Refused

NOTES

Chapter One

1. The records are obvious in the American freshman surveys conducted by the Higher Education Research Institute at the University of California, Los Angeles. In 1997, for example, volunteering hit an all-time high with a record 73.1 percent of college freshmen having performed some kind of volunteer work during their last year in high school. See Linda J. Sax, Alexander W. Astin, William S. Korn, and Kathryn M. Mahoney, *The American Freshman: National Norms for Fall 1997* (University of California, Los Angeles, Higher Education Research Institute, December 1997), p. 4.

2. For an analysis of the relationship between performance and trust, see Pew Research Center for the People and the Press, *Deconstructing Distrust: How Americans View Government* (Washington, 1998). The Pew study showed that ratings of how well government performs were the most significant predictor of trust in government, followed by ratings of the ethical conduct of America's leaders. Whether the statistical relationship has changed since then is not yet known.

3. This is not to discount the number of experiments over the past two decades, but to note that those experiments have generally not taken hold. The classic statement on the need for more aggressive reform comes from the late Charles H. Levine, ed., *The Unfinished Agenda for Civil Service Reform: Implications of the Grace Commission Report* (Brookings, 1985). For a more recent statement, see Donald F. Kettl, Patricia W. Ingraham, Ronald P. Sanders, and Constance Horner, *Civil Service Reform: Building a Government That Works* (Brookings, 1996).

4. The term was invented by Charles H. Levine and Rosslyn S. Kleeman, "The Quiet Crisis in the American Public Service," in Patricia W. Ingraham and Donald F. Kettl, eds., *Agenda for Excellence: Public Service in America* (Chatham, N.J.: Chatham House, 1992).

5. See Paul C. Light, *The True Size of Government* (Brookings, 1999), pp. 85–90, for an analysis of rhetoric toward government in the 1960, 1980, 1992, and 1996 presidential campaigns. Candidate Bill Clinton was particularly attentive to using the word *bureaucracy* instead of *bureaucrats* whenever he criticized big government.

6. National Commission on the Public Service, *Leadership for America: Rebuilding the Public Service, The Report of the National Commission on the Public Service* (Washington, 1989), p. 3.

7. Ibid., p. ix.

8. Donald F. Kettl may have written the definitive analysis of this blurring in *Sharing Power: Public Governance and Private Markets* (Brookings, 1993); for a more recent discussion of various theories of how government employment might change, see Christopher Hood, Desmond King, and B. Guy Peters, "Working for Government: Rival Interpretations of Employment Change in the Public Sector," paper prepared for the annual meeting of the American Political Science Association, Boston, Mass., September 3–6, 1998. For a rival analysis of these arguments, see John D. Donahue, *The Privatization Decision: Public Ends, Private Means* (Basic Books, 1989).

9. William C. Adams and others, "Student Attitudes toward Careers in Public Service," prepared as slide presentation (June 1998), in author's files.

10. Ibid.

11. U.S. Merit Systems Protection Board, *The Changing Federal Workplace: Employee Perspectives* (Washington, 1998).

12. Pew Research Center for the People and the Press, *Public Appetite for Government Misjudged: Washington Leaders Wary of Public Opinion* (Washington, 1998).

13. See Light, *True Size of Government,* for a description of the growing "shadow" of government. While the number of full-time-equivalent jobs purchased from the contracting sector has declined in absolute terms since 1984, the number of jobs purchased under service contracts has grown by one-seventh. Moreover, most of the decline in contract jobs came with Defense downsizing. In 1984, contracting by domestic agencies (excluding NASA and the Department of Energy) purchased roughly 650,000 full-time jobs; by 1996, that number had topped 1 million.

14. William P. Ryan, "The New Landscape for Nonprofits," *Harvard Business Review,* January–February 1999, p. 129.

15. Light, *True Size of Government,* chapters 4 and 5.

16. See Paul C. Light, *Thickening Government: Federal Hierarchy and the Diffusion of Accountability* (Brookings, 1995), p. 192.

17. Light, *True Size of Government,* pp. 125–26.

18. For an excellent example of how such a panel study might be constructed and what this type of study reveals, see M. Kent Jennings and Richard G. Niemi, *Generations and Politics: A Panel Study of Young Adults and their Parents* (Princeton University Press, 1981).

19. The questionnaire design was truly a collaborative effort with colleagues at Princeton Survey Research Associates, particularly principal investigator Mary McIntosh and Christopher Adasiewicz, both of whom added significant value and insight to the effort.

Chapter 2

1. For a remarkably thoughtful analysis of the basic trends that continue to reshape the public service, see Charles H. Levine, "The Federal Government in the Year 2000: Administrative Legacies of the Reagan Years," in Patricia W. Ingraham and Donald F. Kettl, eds., *Agenda for Excellence: Public Service in America* (Chatham, N.J.: Chatham House, 1992). The book was published in honor of Levine following his untimely death in 1988.

2. These figures are from the Pew Research Center for the People and the Press, *Deconstructing Distrust: How Americans View Government* (Washington, 1998), p. 16.

3. Charles T. Goodsell, *The Case for Bureaucracy: A Public Administration Polemic,* 3d ed. (Chatham, N.J.: Chatham House, 1994), pp. 77–78.

4. M. Kent Jennings and Richard Niemi, "The Transmission of Political Values from Parent to Child," *American Political Science Review* vol. 62, no. 1 (March 1968), p. 174.

5. See Paul C. Light, *Baby Boomers* (W. W. Norton, 1988), pp. 180–90, for a discussion of generational party identification.

6 See Kathryn E. Newcomer, "The Changing Nature of Accountability: The Role of the Inspector General in Federal Agencies," *Public Administration Review,* vol. 58, no. 2 (March–April 1998), pp. 129–36.

7. The Reagan quote is from the Inaugural Address of President Ronald Reagan, January 20, 1981; the Gore quote can be found in Al Gore, *From Red Tape to Results: Creating a Government That Works Better & Costs Less,* Report of the National Performance Review (Government Printing Office, 1993), p. 1.

8. Paul C. Light, *The Tides of Reform: Making Government Work, 1945–1995* (Yale University Press, 1997), p. 5.

9. See ibid. for a discussion of the reform movements.

10. Elizabeth G. Chambers and others, "The War for Talent," *McKinsey Quarterly*, No. 3, 1998, pp. 44–57 (http://www.mckinseyquarterly.com/organiz/wata98.htm [May 13, 1999]).

11. Congressional Budget Office, "Comparing Federal Employee Benefits with Those in the Private Sector," August 1998 (http://www.cbo.gov/showdoc.cfm?index=821&sequence=0&from=1 [September 15, 1999]).

12. Katy Saldarini, "In Downsizing, Contractors at DOE Fare Better than Feds," *Government Executive*, June 10, 1999 (http://www.govexec.com/dailyfed/0699/061099k1.htm [September 15, 1999]).

13. See Stephen Barr, "Executives Point to Pay as Problem; Top Managers Difficult to Recruit and Retain," *Washington Post*, June 22, 1999, p. A15.

14. See Bill McAllister, "Shedding Reserve on Defense; OMB to Let Military Contract out Thousands of Jobs," *Washington Post*, June 22, 1999, p. A15.

15. Charles H. Levine and Rosslyn S. Kleeman, "The Quiet Crisis in the American Public Service," in Ingraham and Kettl, *Agenda for Excellence*, p. 265.

16. Joseph Veroff, Elizabeth Douvan, and Richard A. Kulka, *The Inner American: A Self-Portrait from 1957–1976* (Basic Books, 1981), pp. 17–18.

17. Light, *Baby Boomers*, p. 152.

18. Academy for Educational Development, *OurStory: The Public Policy and International Affairs Program* (Washington, 1997).

19. See Walter D. Broadnax and Paul C. Light, "An Environmental Assessment of the Public Policy and International Affairs Program," Report submitted to the Academy for Educational Development, March 1999.

20. Winston J. Allen, *Woodrow Wilson Program in Public Policy and International Affairs: Synthesis Report on Program Evaluation* (Washington: Joint Center for Political and Economic Studies, November 1995).

21. Business majors include accounting/finance, business, and market research; humanities include history, foreign languages, communications, philosophy, religion, and English; political science and law include public administration, law/criminal justice, political science/government/politics, and international relations; sciences include physics, agriculture, biology, engineering, environment, geography, geology, health, and math; social sciences include psychology, sociology, anthropology, economics, urban studies, and social work.

Chapter 3

1. Joseph S. Nye Jr., "The Leadership Brain Drain," *New York Times,* April 5, 1998, p. 46.

2. See William C. Adams and others, "Student Attitudes Toward Careers in Public Service," prepared as slide presentation (June 1998), in author's files.

3. William C. Adams and others, "MPAs and MPPs View Federal Employment: Impressions, Incentives, and Impediments," prepared for submission to the *Journal of Public Administration Education* (1998), p. 17.

4. Jonathan Walters, "Hiring Spree," *Governing*, vol. 11, February 1998, p. 17.

5. These figures are from various editions of the *Statistical Abstract of the United States*.

6. Gabriel Rudney, "The Scope and Dimensions of Nonprofit Activity," in Walter W. Powell, ed., *The Nonprofit Sector: A Research Handbook* (Yale University Press, 1987), p. 57.

7. The 10.2 million figure comes from an update of Virginia A. Hodgkinson, Murray S. Weitzman and Associates, *The Nonprofit Almanac 1996-1997: Dimensions of the Independent Sector* (San Francisco: Jossey-Bass, 1997) provided by Independent Sector at ⟨http://www.indepsec.org/programs/research/update_nonprofit.html [September 18, 1998]⟩.

8. Samatha Stainbum, "Back to School," *Who Cares*, March–April 1998 ⟨http://www.whocares.org/marapr98/cover.htm [September 18, 1999]⟩.

9. Lester M. Salamon, *Holding the Center: America's Nonprofit Sector at a Crossroads* (New York: Nathan Cummings Foundation, 1997), pp. xiii–xviii.

10. National Association of Schools of Public Affairs and Administration, "Make Something Happen with an MPA or MPP," brochure, author's files.

11. The quotations that follow are drawn from program catalogs collected from the Internet and in hard copy. Readers are reminded that some of the programs discussed in this section were not in the survey.

12. At the time of this writing, I am an adjunct professor of practice at the Kennedy School, which may create some bias in this discussion.

13. The thirty-four interviews were conducted in late spring 1999. Respondents were selected at random from the class of 1988 and 1993 respondents who had been interviewed in the earlier telephone survey. The in-depth interviews, conducted by telephone, were recorded and transcribed. My appreciation goes to Nathaniel Balis and Nicole Rawlings of Princeton Survey Research Associates who conducted the in-depth conversations, both of whom created an interview climate that encouraged maximum candor from the respondents.

14. Miles's Law is named for Rufus Miles, a distinguished public administration scholar and government practitioner.

15. H. George Frederickson, *The Spirit of Public Administration* (San Francisco: Jossey-Bass, 1997), p. 179.

16. Because of the small subsample sizes involved in this portion of the analysis, the classes of the 1970s were combined, as were the classes of 1988 and 1993. The class of 1983 is left out of the table.

17. See Paul C. Light, *The Tides of Reform: Making Government Work, 1945–1995* (Yale University Press, 1997), for a discussion of the cumulative frustrations in the constant and contradictory efforts to make government work.

18. Those who have stayed in government throughout their career were less trusting toward their organizations to do the right thing just about always than were those who stayed in the nonprofit or private sector. The figures are 25 percent for government, 34 percent for private, and 44 percent for nonprofit.

19. The study, "Keeping the Keepers: Strategies for Associate Retention in times of Attrition," was conducted by the National Association for Law Placement Foundation for Research and Education (http://www.nalp.org/Trends/keepers.htm [September 18, 1999]).

20. The survey was conducted by UNIVERSUM, a graduate communications consulting firm, and was released on April 29, 1998 (http://www.universum.se/index2.html[May 13, 1999]).

21. Jeffrey Pfeffer, "The Real Cost of the Virtual Workforce," *Stanford Business*, March 1998 (http://www.gsb.stanford.edu/commun...0398/feature_ virtualworkforce.html[October 3, 1999]). This article is an excerpt from Pfeffer's book, *The Human Equation: Building Profits by Putting People First* (Harvard Business School Press, 1998).

22. For a sampling of the growing literature see Vicki Smith, "New Forms of Work Organization," *Annual Review of Sociology* 23 (1997), pp. 315–39; Kevin T. Leicht and Mary L. Fennell, "The Changing Organizational Context of Professional Work," *Annual Review of Sociology* 23 (1997), pp. 215–31;Both articles raise important questions that might shape future research agendas.

23. Because the subsample sizes here are so small, private and nonprofit switchers are combined.

24. Adams and others, "MPAs and MPPs View Federal Employment," p. 17.

Chapter 4

1. This analysis is based on a simple count of the number of core courses required for graduation; it did not weight the number of course credits involved. Unless a given course was clearly identified as a partial course, all courses across the thirteen schools were counted as equal, regardless of the number of credit hours involved.

2. I am grateful to Lisa Zellmer, who collected the course catalogs from the Internet and also identified particularly interesting courses for review. Although her research included the rest of the schools in the top twenty, I have chosen here to focus only on the thirteen schools that participated in the study.

Chapter 5

1. John D. Donahue, *The Privatization Decision: Public Ends, Private Means* (Basic Books, 1989), p. 39.

2. Donald F. Kettl writes about this "fuzzy boundary" problem in his 1998 report, *Reinventing Government: A Fifth-Year Report Card* (Brookings, 1998).

3. For a discussion of the public value concept, see Mark H. Moore, *Creating Public Value: Strategic Management in Government* (Harvard University Press, 1995).

4. I argue that faith, trust, honesty, and rigor are the core values needed for increasing the odds that innovation can occur and endure in public organizations; see Paul C. Light, *Sustaining Innovation: Creating Government and Nonprofit Organizations That Innovate Naturally* (San Francisco: Jossey-Bass, 1998).

5. For further information on this pattern, see Paul C. Light, *The True Size of Government* (Brookings, 1999), pp. 191–94.

6. PricewaterhouseCoopers has created a separate funding program to support research and conferences on public service, for example. Called the PricewaterhouseCoopers Endowment for Business in Government, it is the most important small grants program currently open to scholars of public administration.

INDEX

Adams, William C., 45
African American graduates, 31, 83–84, 100–01
Agriculture, U.S. Department of, 10, 49
Allison, Graham, 54
Alumni networks, 123–24
American Society of Public Administration, 123
American University, 53
Appointed positions in federal government, 2; job satisfaction, 5–6; number of, 10; titles, 9, 10–11
Arthur Andersen, 51
Asian American graduates, 31
Association for Public Policy Analysis and Management, 135

Baby boom generation: attitudes toward work, 27, 82; loyalty to employers, 82; party identification, 22; political socialization, 22; upcoming retirements, 24
Booz-Allen and Hamilton, 51

Boston Consulting Group, 80
Bureaucracy: in private sector, 74–75. *See also* Government
Bureau of Land Management, 10
Bush administration, 9
Business. *See* Private sector
Business schools: job switching by graduates, 80; joint degree programs, 104; nonprofit management programs, 41, 50, 135

California, University of (Berkeley), 122
Careers. *See* Public service careers
Carnegie Mellon University, Heinz School of Public Policy and Management, 15, 16, 57; career options, 55; career paths of graduates, 84; core curriculum, 113; courses, 57, 120, 121–22; undergraduate majors of students, 34
Catholic Charities, 7
Census Bureau, 49
Centers for Disease Control, 20
Central Intelligence Agency, 20

Change: managing, 112, 121–22

Chicago, University of, Harris School, 15, 16; career paths of graduates, 84; focus on government careers, 58; preparation for nonprofit careers, 122; preparation for private sector careers, 55, 114, 119; undergraduate majors of students, 34

City managers, 47. *See also* Local government

Civil service. *See* Government

Civil Service Reform Act, 3, 136

Clinton, Bill: cuts in federal employment, 10, 12–13, 23; scandals, 21

Clinton administration: number of senior executives in government, 9; titles of senior executives, 10–11

Commerce, U.S. Department of, 10, 11

Communications technology, 119, 121, 134

Comprehensive public policy and administration graduate schools, 16; career options, 56–57; career paths of graduates, 82–83. *See also* Public policy and administration graduate schools

Confidence in government, 19–20, 21–22, 62, 63–66, 127–28

Conflict management skills, 109, 117, 118, 120–21, 134

Congress: attempts to reform government, 23–24; job satisfaction of members, 5–6; military base closings, 10

Congressional Budget Office, 24–25

Consulting firms: business school graduates hired by, 80; courses preparing for work in, 119; growth of government practice, 126; jobs in, 48, 51, 84

Contractors. *See* Outsourcing

Corrections Corporation of America, 7

Corrections officers, 7, 50

Cultural change, 26–27

Dade County (Fla.), 7

Defense, U.S. Department of: contract work force, 8, 25; military base closings, 10; public confidence in, 20; work force, 7

Deloitte and Touche, 51, 84

Democratic party, 22, 40

Demographic trends, 28; diverse work force, 32, 109, 122, 127; diversity of graduates, 29, 30–34, 41, 83–84; labor shortages, 24, 26

Donahue, John D., 129–30

Douvan, Elizabeth, 26–27

Downsizing: of federal government, 4, 5, 7, 8, 10, 12–13, 49, 129–30; in private sector, 25, 74, 75, 92

Duke University, Terry Sanford Institute of Public Policy, 55–56

Education, U.S. Department of, 10, 20

Employee benefits: as criterion for job, 31–32, 39, 96, 137; in government, 24–25, 45, 137; in private sector, 24–25

Employees. *See* Federal government employees; Government employees; Jobs; Nonprofit sector; Private sector

Employers: lack of loyalty to employees, 92; loyalty to, 77–78, 80, 82. *See also* Downsizing; Jobs; Recruiting

Emulation, law of, 11, 74

Energy, U.S. Department of, 10, 11, 25

Environmental Protection Agency, 10, 20, 49

Ethics: courses, 111, 120; difficulty of teaching, 110; importance of maintaining standards, 109, 110, 117, 120; learning, 117–18

Federal Aviation Administration, 10
Federal Emergency Management Agency, 49
Federal government: changing shape of hierarchy, 8, 9–10, 11–13; contract work force, 7, 8–9, 12–13, 25, 26, 93, 130; devolution of responsibilities to state and local government, 7; effects of constant reform and reinvention, 65–66; layers of hierarchy, 10–11; privatization of functions, 93; public confidence in, 19–20, 21–22; public view of performance, 20; reform and reinvention efforts, 6, 21, 22, 23–24, 25, 65–66, 112; scandals, 21; shutdowns, 5; war on waste, 22–23, 65–66. *See also* Government; *and specific departments and agencies*
Federal government employees: appointed positions, 2, 5–6, 10; benefits, 24–25, 45, 137; confidence in government, 65, 127–28; downsizing of work force, 4, 5, 7, 8, 10, 12–13, 49, 129–30; first jobs of graduates, 43, 57, 61; increased average grade, 12; job satisfaction, 5–6; job security, 45, 97, 99; lower-level jobs eliminated, 8, 12–13; middle-level managers, 8, 9–10, 11–13; morale, 5; Presidential Management Internships, 58, 87, 136; reasons for taking jobs, 45–46; recruiting difficulties, 25; retention difficulties, 25; salaries, 25; senior executives, 4–6, 9, 10–11, 25, 136; titles, 9, 10–11

Federal Inspector General Act, 23
Federalist Papers, The, 2
Federal Yellow Book, 9
First jobs of graduates: criteria in choice of, 94–97; differences by type of program, 46–48; differences in switching behavior, 46, 48–49, 84–88, 128, 131, 132; expectations, 36–37; in government, 43, 46, 47–48, 57, 61, 126; importance of choice, 132–33; in nonprofit sector, 45, 46, 57, 61, 87–88, 126, 128; in private sector, 45, 46, 48, 57, 61, 84, 126, 128
Food and Drug Administration, 20
Ford Foundation, 30, 32, 34
Fraud investigations, 23, 65–66
Frederickson, George, 62, 120
Fund-raising skills, 109, 117, 122

Gender. *See* Men; Women
General Accounting Office, 10
General Services Administration, 10
George Washington University, 5, 13, 45
Georgia, University of, 53
Gooding, Cuba Jr., 46
Goodsell, Charles, 21
Gore, Albert Jr., 6, 21, 22, 23
Governing, 49
Government: attitudes of graduates toward, 62, 63–66, 67, 68–70, 127–28, 132; competition for talent with other sectors, 1–3, 25, 26, 46, 86–87, 97, 98–99, 135–39, 141; demand for labor, 49–51; desire to keep small, 125–26; difficulty of entering in mid-career, 86, 87, 99, 132, 137–38; human resource offices, 138; lack of interest in employment, 4–5, 43–46; need for talented employees, 2; prior experi-

ence of graduates, 38, 39; problems in recruiting and retaining employees, 2, 3–5, 68–70, 85, 86–87, 129, 136–39; public's view of, 2, 19–21; recommended changes, 135–39; slow decisionmaking, 68. *See also* Federal government; Local government; State government

Government employees: ability to make large impact, 67, 97, 98; effects of leadership changes, 68; entry-level jobs, 86–87; internal promotions, 69, 86, 87, 137; job satisfaction, 5–6, 79, 88, 132–33; job security, 45, 97, 98, 99, 137; motives for working in government, 67, 89–91, 98, 132–33, 137; public's view of, 19–20, 68; reasons for leaving government, 68, 69, 89–90; recruiting, 86–87, 136–39; retaining, 85, 87, 138–39; switching to other sectors, 46, 61, 68, 69, 84–85, 89–90, 128; unclear criteria for advancement, 69; value of graduate degree, 105–06. *See also* Federal government employees

Graduates. *See* Public policy and administration graduates

Graduate schools. *See* Public policy and administration graduate schools

Hamilton, Alexander, 2

Harris School. *See* Chicago, University of

Harvard University, Kennedy School, 15, 16; career options, 56–57, 58; career paths of graduates, 84; core curriculum, 111, 113; courses, 111, 120; first jobs of graduates, 45, 57; graduates in nonprofit sector, 45;

mid-career students, 38, 56–57; motives of students, 94; nonprofit concentration offered, 52, 57, 119–20; undergraduate majors of students, 34; work experience of students, 38

Health, Education, and Welfare, U.S. Department of, 49

Health care employment, 50

Heinz School of Public Policy and Management. *See* Carnegie Mellon University

Hispanic graduates, 31, 101

Housing and Urban Development, U.S. Department of, 10, 49

Human resource offices, in government agencies, 138

Humphrey Institute. See Minnesota, University of

Indiana University, 15, 16; career paths of graduates, 84; courses, 121; undergraduate majors of students, 34

Information technology management, 118, 119, 121, 134

Inspectors general, 23

Interior, U.S. Department of, 10

Internal Revenue Service, 20

Internship programs, 58, 87, 136

Jennings, M. Kent, 22

Jobs: commitment to, 27; criteria in choice of, 3, 37, 39, 59, 67, 94–98, 137; graduates' current, 43–45, 61, 78–79, 88, 93, 96–97, 99–101. *See also* First jobs; Salaries; Switching sectors

Job satisfaction, 99–101; of Congress members, 5–6; of government employees, 5–6, 79, 88, 132–33; of

graduates in current jobs, 78–79, 88, 93, 99–101; in nonprofit sector, 79, 99; in private sector, 79; racial and ethnic differences, 100–01; relationship to career path, 88, 93, 100; relationship to salary, 101
Job security: as criterion for job, 31–32, 39, 96; in government, 45, 97, 98, 99, 137. *See also* Downsizing
Johnson School. *See* Texas, University of
Joint Center for Political and Economic Studies, 33
Justice, U.S. Department of, 9–10, 49

Kansas, University of, Edwin O. Stene Graduate Program in Public Administration, 15, 16; careers of graduates, 47, 53, 84; core curriculum, 113, 114; ethics courses, 111, 120; focus on local government, 47, 53, 62; undergraduate majors of students, 34
Kennedy School of Government. *See* Harvard University
Kleeman, Rosslyn S., 26
Kulka, Richard, 26–27

Labor, U.S. Department of, 10
Labor market: changes in, 24, 49, 80–81; diverse work force, 32, 109, 122; government demand, 49–51; shortages, 24, 26
Ladd, Helen F., 55–56
Latinos. *See* Hispanic graduates
Law schools: job switching by graduates, 80; joint degree programs, 104, 114
LBJ School. *See* Texas, University of
Leadership skills: courses, 111, 120; difficulty of teaching, 110; impor-

tance of, 109, 110, 117; learning, 117–18
Levine, Charles H., 26
Local government: city managers, 47; confidence in, 65; contracts with private firms, 7, 136; demand for labor, 49–50; devolution of responsibilities to, 7; first jobs of graduates in, 43, 57, 61; skills needed, 109; training for, 47, 53. *See also* Government
Lockheed Martin, 7, 51

Managers: middle-level in government, 8, 9–10, 11–13; skills needed, 32, 109, 112, 121–22, 122
Maximus, 7, 51
Maxwell School of Citizenship and Public Affairs. *See* Syracuse University
MBA programs. *See* Business schools
McKinsey and Company, 80
McKinsey Quarterly, 24
Media relations, 119
Men: career paths, 83; goals in public service careers, 29–30; work experience in government, 29; work experience in nonprofit sector, 29
Merit Systems Protection Board, 5, 13
Michigan, University of, 15, 16; career paths of graduates, 84; core curriculum, 113; courses, 111, 120, 121; undergraduate majors of students, 34
Microeconomics, 43, 115, 116
Miles's Law, 62, 65, 112
Military base closings, 10
Minnesota, University of, Humphrey Institute, 15, 16; career options, 54, 56; career paths of graduates, 84; core curriculum, 117; focus on gov-

ernment careers, 58; joint degree programs, 114; preparation for nonprofit sector, 57, 116–17, 122; undergraduate majors of students, 34

Mirabella, Roseanne, 50
Moe, Ronald, 54
Moynihan, Daniel Patrick, 11, 74

National Aeronautics and Space Administration (NASA), 10, 49
National Association of Schools of Public Affairs and Administration (NASPAA), 52, 135
National Commission on the Public Service, 3–4
National Park Service, 20
Negotiation skills, 121
Niemi, Richard, 22
Nonprofit management: business school programs, 41, 50, 135; courses, 45, 50, 52, 55, 57, 120, 121, 122; programs, 52, 57, 119–20; skills needed, 110, 112, 116–17
Nonprofit Management Education in the Year 2000, 50
Nonprofit sector: attitudes of graduates toward, 62, 66, 69, 70–72, 127; career motivations of graduates, 39; commitment to, 39, 42, 70, 71, 142; competition from private sector, 50–51; contracts to deliver government services, 7, 50, 92; crisis of 1990s, 50–51; employment growth, 50, 126; first jobs in, 45, 46, 57, 61, 87–88, 126, 128; funders, 139–40; fund-raising pressure, 71–72, 122; high turnover, 71, 72, 102, 139; increased number of organizations, 139, 140; interest in employment in, 5, 31–32, 45,

87–88; job satisfaction, 79, 99; likelihood of returning after graduate school, 39; motives for working in, 90, 98; prior experience of graduates, 29, 38, 39; problems of careers in, 71–72; reasons to leave, 72, 90–91; retaining employees, 139–40; strengths, 62; stress, 91, 102, 131, 139; switching from, 46, 72, 84, 85, 86, 88, 90–91, 131; uncertain future, 102; value of graduate degree, 105–06, 116–17; women in, 29
North Carolina, University of, 15, 16; career paths of graduates, 84; conflict management course, 120–21; undergraduate majors of students, 34
Nye, Joseph S., 45, 57

Occupational Safety and Health Administration, 49
O'Connell, Brian, 54
Office of Management and Budget, 12
Office of Personnel Management, 3, 10, 93
Organizational diagnosis, 135
Outsourcing, 26, 125–26, 127, 129–30; at federal level, 7, 8–9, 25, 26, 93; lack of tracking at federal level, 12; to nonprofit organizations, 7, 50, 92; to private sector, 6, 7, 51, 59, 60, 92–93; public service obligations of private firms, 140–41; at state and local levels, 7, 92–93, 136

Pennsylvania, University of, 51
Pfeffer, Jeffrey, 80
Policy analysis: importance of skill, 115, 116–17, 131, 134; methods taught in graduate schools, 43, 113, 114–15

Policy analysis schools, 16; career paths of graduates, 82–83; emphasis on quantitative methods, 35, 113; first jobs of graduates, 47, 48; preparation for private sector careers, 54–56. *See also* Public policy and administration graduate schools

Political independents, 22, 40

Political parties: identification with, 22, 27, 40

Political socialization, 22

PPIA (Public Policy and International Affairs) program, 32–34

Presidential Management Internships, 58, 87, 136

PricewaterhouseCoopers, 25, 51

Princeton Survey Research Associates, 15, 16

Princeton University, 51

Prison guards, 7, 50

Private sector: attitudes of graduates toward, 58–61, 62, 72–74, 90, 91, 127; bureaucracy in, 74–75; career motivations of graduates, 39; comparative advantage over other sectors, 97–98; competition with nonprofit sector, 50–51; contracts to deliver government services, 6, 7, 51, 59, 60, 92–93; criticism of careers in, 59, 60–61, 69, 70–71, 74–75; downsizing in, 25, 74, 75, 92; employee benefits, 24–25; first jobs in, 45, 46, 48, 57, 61, 84, 126, 128; graduate school preparation, 45, 53–56, 114, 119; interest in employment in, 5, 45, 51, 73, 75, 84, 91, 98–99, 130; job satisfaction, 79; prior experience of graduates, 38, 39; profit motive, 60–61, 69, 70–71; public service aspects of jobs, 59, 60–61, 76; public service

obligations, 62, 140–41; reasons to leave, 70–71, 90–91; recruiting employees, 6, 42, 51, 129, 140; salaries, 25, 51, 75, 84, 90, 97–98, 99; skills necessary for careers in, 45; switching from, 46, 70–71, 84, 85, 86, 90–91; value of experience in, 59, 60; value of graduate degree, 105–06. *See also* Consulting firms

Privatization. *See* Outsourcing

Public: confidence in government, 19–20, 21–22, 62, 65–66, 127–28; view of government, 2, 19–21; view of government employees, 19–20, 68

Public administration schools, 16; career paths of graduates, 82–83; first jobs of graduates, 46–47, 48; focus on government careers, 48–49, 52–53; number of students, 35. *See also* Public policy and administration graduate schools

Public policy and administration graduates: academic backgrounds, 34–37; additional graduate degrees, 103, 133; alumni networks, 123–24; attitudes toward government, 62, 63–66, 67, 68–70, 127–28, 132; attitudes toward nonprofit sector, 62, 66, 69, 70–72, 127; attitudes toward private sector, 58–61, 62, 69, 72–74, 90, 91, 127; career goals, 36–37, 45–46; career trends, 126–27; changes in public service during careers of, 21–28; classes, 14–15; commitment to public service, 94–96, 128–29, 142; current jobs, 43–45, 61, 78–79, 88, 93, 96–97, 99–101; declining interest in government careers, 43–46; demographics, 29–34, 41; gender differences, 29–30, 41, 83; histories, 28–29, 34–37; mid-career students, 37, 38, 41, 56–57; motivations for getting degree, 103; ongoing learning, 117–18, 133; political views, 22, 27, 40; racial and ethnic differences, 30–34, 41, 83–84, 100–01; satisfaction with graduate schools, 42, 43, 103–08, 115–17, 133–34; skills considered important, 30, 32, 108–12, 114–17; study of, 13–17; undergraduate majors, 34–37; views of different sectors, 5, 62–76, 127–28; work experience, 29, 31, 37–39, 130. *See also* First jobs; Switching sectors

Public policy and administration graduate schools: acceptance of changes in public service, 52–57; associations, 52, 135; bias toward government careers, 53, 58, 62; career planning assistance, 124, 134; competition from business schools, 41; comprehensive schools, 16, 56–57, 82–83; core curriculums, 35, 36, 41, 43, 111, 113–15, 117, 119, 134; curriculum suggestions, 108–12, 118–23, 134; differences between public and private, 84; difficulty of teaching students with diverse academic backgrounds, 106–07, 115; innovative courses, 119–23, 134; institutes for students of color, 32–34; joint degree programs, 104, 114; lack of prerequisites, 36, 41; lengths of programs, 114, 115; non-profit management courses and programs, 45, 50, 52, 55, 57, 116–17, 119–20, 121, 122; policy analysis schools, 16, 35, 47, 48, 54–56, 82–83, 113; preparation for private sector careers, 45, 53–56, 114, 119; private firms recruiting at, 6, 42, 51, 129, 140; public administration schools, 16, 35, 46–47, 48–49, 52–53, 82–83; satisfaction of graduates, 42, 43, 103–08, 115–17, 133–34; teaching methods, 104; top twenty, 14, 15–16. *See also* Skills

Public Policy and International Affairs (PPIA) program, 32–34

Public service: changes in, 1–2, 6–9, 21–28, 49–51, 101; commitment to, 28, 77, 94–96, 128–29, 142; different strengths of sectors, 61–67; diversity of, 127; lack of interest in, 4–5; movement of jobs from government to nonprofit and private sectors, 7, 12–13, 26, 48–49, 92–93, 125–26, 127, 129–30; public's expectations of, 21; quiet crisis in, 3–4; uncertain future, 101–02. *See also* Government; Nonprofit sector; Private sector

Public service careers: changing nature of, 13; criteria in choice of jobs, 3, 37, 39, 96–97, 137; gender differences in goals, 29–30; interest in, 2–3; racial differences in goals, 31–32; single employer, 77–78; views of students, 1. *See also* First jobs; Jobs; Switching sectors

Quantitative methods: debate over importance of, 107, 114–15; focus on in core curriculums, 35, 43, 113, 117, 134; importance of skills, 131, 134; skills not prerequisites for graduate school, 36, 41, 107–08, 115

Reagan, Ronald, 23
Reagan administration, 9, 23, 48
Recruiting: difficulties of government, 2, 3–5, 25, 68–70, 85, 86–87, 129,

136–38; by private firms, 6, 42, 51, 129, 140

Reinventing government program, 21, 22, 23, 65–66, 112

Republican party, 22, 40

Ryan, William, 7

Salamon, Lester M., 50, 51, 66

Salaries: at consulting firms, 51, 84; as criterion for job, 31–32, 40, 59, 75, 90, 96, 97–98, 137; in federal government, 25; less important than other criteria, 3, 37, 45–46, 70, 96; in private sector, 25, 51, 75, 84, 90, 97–98, 99; relationship to job satisfaction, 101

San Diego (Calif.), 7

Sanford Institute. See Duke University

Senior Executive Service, 5–6, 136

Skills: common needs of different sectors, 112; conflict management, 109, 117, 118, 120–21, 134; considered important by graduates, 30, 32, 108–12, 114–17; differences by sector, 117; fund raising, 109, 117, 122; gaps in teaching of, 115–17; improving teaching of, 108–12, 115–17, 134–35; information technology management, 118, 119, 121, 134; knowledge of other sectors, 131, 134; leadership, 109, 110, 111, 117–18, 120; maintaining ethical standards, 109, 110, 117–18, 120; managing diverse work force, 32, 109, 122; managing innovation and change, 112, 121–22; media relations, 119; organizational diagnosis, 135; policy analysis, 43, 113, 114–15, 116–17, 131, 134; taught by graduate schools, 43, 113–18. See also Quantitative methods

Sloan Foundation, 30, 32

Social Security Administration, 10

Social services: nonprofit providers, 7, 50, 92; private contractors, 7, 51, 92–93

Southern California, University of, 15, 16; career paths of graduates, 84; core curriculum, 113; courses, 111, 121; undergraduate majors of students, 34

State, U.S. Department of, 9–10, 49

State government: confidence in, 65; contracts with private firms, 7, 92–93, 136; demand for labor, 49–50; devolution of responsibilities to, 7; first jobs of graduates in, 43, 57, 61; negative views of, 68. See also Government

State University of New York, Albany, 15, 16; career paths of graduates, 84; courses, 122; undergraduate majors of students, 34

Stene Graduate Program in Public Administration. See Kansas, University of

Students: advice to, 130–32; diverse academic backgrounds, 106–07, 115; interest in government employment, 45; interest in private and nonprofit sectors, 45; lack of interest in government employment, 4–5; specialization, 131–32; views of careers, 1. See also Public policy and administration graduates

Swangstue, Shannon, 93

Switching sectors, 48–49, 76; barriers, 86, 87, 99; career paths, 81; differences between public and private schools, 84; differences between types of schools, 82–83; differences related to first jobs, 46, 48–49, 84–88, 128, 131, 132; extent of,

76; gender differences, 83; from
government, 46, 61, 68, 69, 84–85,
89–90; increasing rate of, 46, 102,
128; intentions, 76–81, 91–92, 93;
life-cycle effects, 76–77, 81–82, 85;
motives, 88–93; from nonprofit sector, 46, 72, 84, 85, 86, 88, 90–91,
131; not related to undergraduate
major, 36; from private sector, 46,
70–71, 84, 85, 86, 90–91; racial
differences, 83–84; rates, 46,
81–84, 102, 128; relationship to
job satisfaction, 88, 93, 100; as
result of outsourcing, 92–93
Syracuse University, Maxwell School of
Citizenship and Public Affairs, 15,
16, 53–54; career options, 58; career
paths of graduates, 84; core curriculum, 113; courses, 111, 121; joint
degree programs, 104; mid-career
students, 37, 38; preparation for private sector careers, 119; recruiting
by private firms, 51; undergraduate
majors of students, 34

Teachers, 49–50
Technology: effects of changes, 28;
information technology management skills, 118, 119, 121, 134;
jobs eliminated by, 8
Texas, University of, Johnson School,
15, 16; career options, 56, 58;
career paths of graduates, 84;
courses, 120, 122; undergraduate
majors of students, 34
Transportation, U.S. Department of,
10
Treasury, U.S. Department of, 10

U.S. government. *See* Federal govern-
ment; *and specific departments and
agencies*
U.S. Investigation Service, 93
U.S. News and World Report, 14
U.S. Postal Service, 19–20
United Way, 50

Veroff, Joseph, 26–27
Volcker, Paul, 3

Washington, University of, 15, 16;
career paths of graduates, 84;
undergraduate majors of students,
34
Washington Post, 25
Waste in government, 22–23, 65–66
Welfare-to-work services, 7, 92
Whites: career paths, 83–84; job satisfaction, 101
Wisconsin, University of: La Follette
Institute, 54–55
Women: career paths, 83; goals in
public service careers, 29–30; public
policy and administration graduates, 29–30, 41; work experience in
government, 29; work experience in
nonprofit sector, 29
Work experience before graduate
school, 37–39; gender differences,
29; racial differences, 31; relationship to career motivations, 39; relationship to later careers, 39; relationship to views of sectors, 130
Workforce Restructuring Act, 10, 12,
49

Yale University, 55